The Broken Fountain

The Broken Fountain

Thomas Belmonte

SECOND EXPANDED EDITION

Columbia University Press
New York

Frontispiece by Jusepe de Ribera, Musée du Louvre, Paris, reproduced by courtesy of cliché des Musées Nationaux, Paris.

Columbia University Press
New York   Chichester, West Sussex

Copyright © 1979, 1989 Columbia University Press
All rights reserved
Library of Congress Cataloging-in-Publication Data
Belmonte, Thomas, 1946–
The broken fountain.
Bibliiography: p. Includes index.
1. Naples (Italy)—Social conditions.
2. Poor—Italy—Naples—Case studies.
3. Family—Italy—Naples—Case studies.
I. Title.
HN488.N3B4 1989 306'.0945'73 89-9883
ISBN 0-231-07058-6
ISBN 0-231-07059-4 (pbk.)

Printed in the United States of America

Casebound editions of Columbia University Press books are
Smyth-sewn and printed on permanent and durable acid-free
paper.

p 10 9 8 7

To Gitel, who is gone now
and to Christina, who becomes

contents

preface ————————————————————————

EVERYONE HAS PERHAPS seen those examples of anamorphic art, which engage the viewer with a seemingly inexplicable optical mystery. As a child, I recall being intrigued by an inexpensive print that hung in the hallway of my parent's home—a drawing of a young woman seated in front of a mirror. When regarded from another angle, this innocent portrait transformed itself into the chilling figure of a human skull. Contemplating it, I would blink my eyes repeatedly so as to summon forth the contrasting images in rapid alternation. But sometimes one of the images would remain stubbornly in place and no amount of blinking would bring the other into view. Then I would turn away, troubled and confused, not certain whether I or the print was to blame.

I think that some levels of social reality present similar dilemmas of perception and confidence to anthropological fieldworkers in foreign lands. I confess that I was baffled by the Neapolitans among whom I lived. No sooner would I discern a pattern in the chaos of shapes confronting me, than the design would rearrange itself into what looked like something else. In those rarer intervals when the line did not waver, I would scrutinize and mistrust it and wonder what was wrong.

The fieldworker lives among individuals, surrounded by the profusion of their idiosyncracies, and yet from his

knowledge of their lives he must abstract "social organization" and write down in his notebooks the prescriptions of
culture. But individuals do not simply receive and spout
out a cultural legacy. They live with it and through it, suffering it or evading it, perhaps even creating it at critical
psychohistorical junctures. The problem posed by Yeats
and revived critically by Kenneth Burke still remains:
"How can we know the dancer from the dance?"[1] For all
our increasing sophistication as social scientists, as plot-
ters and analysts of behavior, we have yet to demonstrate
how the rather stolid architecture of culture houses the
anarchy of motives which is perhaps the essence of human
experience.

When we study human beings we risk a problematical
relationship with them. As in all other human relationships, a stance of pure objectivity (eliminating the self) is
as destructive to communication as is a stance of pure subjectivity (eliminating the other). If cultural anthropology
ceases to rely for insight upon an ongoing dialogue in
which subject and object constantly change places and re-
verse roles, it will become a barren technic, a dried husk
of what C. Wright Mills called "abstracted empiricism."[2]

Although this study seeks to explore an ethnographic
frontier, it does not pretend to do so in a theoretical or a
moral-philosophical vacuum. The data is presented and
analyzed in a mode consistent with the author's reading of
history and provisional understanding of social structure.
This view emphasizes the emergence of stratification as
the pivot upon which all recent history turns and sees
wealth, poverty, and alienation as the crucial components
of a complex cybernetic process.

The method of field research was pure participant observation and is described in greater detail in the first
chapter. I learned about lower-class Neapolitans by living
with them. I came to know them slowly and haltingly. As

they gradually put more trust in me, they let me know them better. My approach was not to dig and hunt for data, in structured, methodical ways, but to watch for it and to wait for it, as I navigated my way through what was essentially an exotic milieu. Participant observation was a means to an end, but it was also an end in itself. It was an immersion in otherness, a prolonged listening, an alteration of self.

The method has conditioned the result, expanding some horizons and limiting others. The book concentrates primarily on those arenas of social life to which I had access in an all too brief year of field research. These are economy, community, and family. Politics is dealt with in summary fashion, while religion, education, the media, and other areas of culture (such as folklore and music) are not treated in any systematic way. I regret these lacunae but hope that others will aid me in filling them in. I think it important that a majority of my informants were male. Nevertheless, I do not think that the view of social life presented here is invalidated by this fact, although a complementary study from the female side of the system would certainly go far toward rounding out our understanding of social life among the Neapolitan poor.

Finally, I would caution the reader that he or she will find no neatly prepared and preserved specimen in the pages that follow. I have made no attempt to drain the blood out of the individuals and scenes, the fears, the conflicts, and the pleasures by which my knowledge of social life among the Neapolitan poor was gained.

acknowledgments

A BOOK, IF it is to be more than a manual or a bulletin, must always manifest the peculiar quality of the author's life as it has involved others. As I read through these pages I see, as the reader cannot, the faces of teachers and friends who encouraged and challenged me and sometimes winced. Had they not cared about this project, I know that I should never have completed it.

First thanks go to my mother and father, Vito and Theodora Belmonte, who never questioned the arduous and strange manner of my return to the land of our ancestors. Always somewhere in the background, silently, they stood by me from start to finish, and for this I am deeply grateful.

As an anthropologist I have been fortunate in having had fine teachers. This book, I hope, will reflect the spirit of the anthropology which they taught me. Alexander Lesser, by his own example, taught me a science which was objective and compassionate at once; and up until her recent death, Gitel Steed provided a spiritual hearth and gave generously the solace of her wisdom. At Columbia University I was apprenticed to the master craftsmen of my profession. From Conrad Arensberg I learned how to appreciate the manifold intricacies of culture history, while searching for order and broad pattern in human affairs. Morton Fried tutored me in political economy and

xiii

grounded my understandings in a materialism that was effortlessly a humanism. Robert Murphy stood everything else I had learned on its head, exposing in his subtle paradoxes the tragicomedies of social life and individual destiny. To these dear teachers, I must acknowledge lifelong debts of heart and mind.

I would also like to thank Herbert Gans and Maristella Lorch of Columbia University, whose presence enlivened my doctoral defense and whose comments have improved the final product. Let me here salute John Moore and Maria Caliandro of the Columbia University Press, who have helped me to smooth and polish at least some of the rough edges.

How can I thank my friends, who read my work when it was raw and crude, and valued it, and helped me to refine its sentences and notions. I am grateful to Saio Adrian, practical humanist, whose comments have forced me throughout to an understanding of the difference between the presentation of the data and the attainment of a sympathetic understanding. Ida Susser, Neil Foran, Kathy MacArdle, John Kreniske, Leni Silverstein, Diane Losche, and Glenn Petersen provided vital support and aid, emotional and editorial, at various stages. Katha Pollitt, Bette Denich, and Muriel Dimen-Schein were kind enough to criticize different sections of the manuscript. I would like to extend special thanks to William Kass for rare gifts of good counsel and continuing faith.

In Naples many helped. I regret that I cannot name them all here. But to my dear friends in Naples, who helped me to know their city and ferried me across its terrible divisions of power and wealth, I acknowledge profound gratitude. More than anyone else, Pietro Radice shared throughout in the frustrations and occasional triumphs that accompany the ethnographic enterprise. He and Pasquale Matera guided me through a complex and sometimes dangerous social labyrinth. The affable companionship of Paolo Sessa was respite and refuge for me, while in the beginning Antonio Marotta provided a gracious and warm introduction to the life of the polis.

I also wish to thank Antonio Vitiello of the University of Naples for his kind offer of hospitality and assistance in the early phase of my research.

My return trip to Naples in 1983–84 was funded by a grant from the National Endowment for the Humanities. In the course of that year, I was the beneficiary of both the assistance and warm hospitality of Marino Niola and Marina Tagliapietra, of Gianni Laino and Anna Stanco, of Donatella Mazzoleni, Tullio Tentori, Cora Hahn, and John Salamack. Once more, the friendship of Pietro Radice and Pasquale Matera sustained me throughout the year but especially when crossing over the dark and barren terrain. On this side of the Atlantic, I would like to renew my gratitude to William Kass, Neil Foran, Ida Susser, and John Kreniske. At Hofstra University, the unflagging support of my colleagues Solomon Miller and Cheryl Mwaria has been crucial. I would like to again thank Saio Adrian for the accuracy and acuity of his editorial judgments and to acknowledge the encouragement and support of James Aust.

Finally, to the people of the place I call Fontana del Re, I am always grateful. I hope they will recognize themselves here and not frown at the portraits contained inside. Perhaps they will recall, out of a past which for me does not fade, that strange and frightened American who has walked among them over the years.

Introduction: The Broken Fountain in Retrospect

IN ENGLISH, THE verb "to know" can refer to a knower's cognitive register of objects, events and of their causal relations *and* to a knower's personal knowledge of self and other. In many other languages, including Italian, a distinction must be made between that knowledge that issues directly from the involvement of the person in the world and that knowledge that is objectively separable from the central core of one's subjectivity. One can merely "know about" something or one can "know with." Once a speaker has internalized the two forms of the verb "to know," the limitations of only using one form are felt acutely. But what is more interesting is that, in terms of linguistic etiquettes, it is more acceptable to progress from the isolation and distance of, for example, "sapere" to the more social and proximate "conoscere" than it is to move in the other direction. The knower's movement can only be from narrowness to fullness, from part to whole. Once attained, knowledge of the whole cannot be undone. Even psychoanalysis was founded on the futility of ever achieving merely objective knowledge of what one had once loved. But whereas psychoanalysis finds its methodological pivot in the concept of the transference, anthropology is not so frank in acknowledging and building upon its bondage to the yearnings of persons. Strange words like "fieldwork," "the field" and "informant" tell of our ruses and our fears.

Introduction: The Broken Fountain in Retrospect

The Broken Fountain is an ethnographic text conceived in the "conoscere" mode, that of "knowing with" as opposed to "knowing about." The hidden sources of whatever authority it possesses derive, following James Clifford's critical project, from the reader's faith in the experience of the ethnographer-as-writer, and from the narratives, the dialogues, the reproduced conversations, and their ultimate interpretations in the context of contemporary social theory.[1]

I once heard a folk healer give his advice on how to insure good nutrition: "Stick to the foods that have the most life in them!" In the writing and the reading of both literature and ethnography that rule will serve us well. Consider D. H. Lawrence's reflections on the novel. A novel that fulfilled the potentials of the genre had to be above all, (1) quick (alive), (2) interrelated in all of its parts, and (3) honorable, i.e., honest about its own pretensions. The didactic purposes and philosophical biases of novelists (Lawrence called all of them "dribbling liars") weighed the novel down and subverted its mission of revealing a pattern of relationships. For Lawrence, the novel was the highest form of human expression "because it is so incapable of the absolute."[2]

Ethnographers as well as novelists would do well to heed Lawrence's injunctions *not* to yield to the temptations of mere theory ("Stick to the life.") When, in 1983, I returned to Naples for a year of additional research, I was deeply committed to the purposes of theoretical anthropology. I very much wanted to "wrap up" my experience of Naples in terms that would be anthropologically "absolute." In the course of pursuing this goal, I became aware, at first subliminally and then consciously, of feelings that, under other circumstances, I would have identified as guilt. When I departed from Naples in 1975, I had come to know many people in their fullness as persons. In 1983, I learned, there would be no "going back" to some narrower vision of them as actors in a scenario written and directed by a social scientist. Until I realized this, I could neither obtain knowledge of the other nor render it accurately (faithfully). The epilogue to the present edition documents some of the necessarily mixed emotions that attended this phase of my ethnographic odyssey.

But to admit to the personal terms and conditions that enable the acquisition of anthropological knowledge is not to demote the status or diminish the utility of that knowledge. Whether we operate with a scientific apparatus that seeks to prove or in an artistic, intuitive mode that seeks to reveal, our goals converge when we discover patterns of relationship and interconnectedness, especially those patterns that either enhance the processes of life and health or weaken and destroy them. I would like to take this opportunity to briefly comment upon the sorts of human relationships which *The Broken Fountain* is at pains to reveal. Of course, I make no claims for proof.

In 1899, W.E.B. DuBois gave what is still the most incisive summation of what a *complete* study of any oppressed group should entail. "A complete study," he wrote, "must not confine itself to the group, but must specially notice the environment, the physical environment of city, sections, and houses, the far mightier social environment—the surrounding world of custom, wish, whim and thought which envelopes this group and powerfully influences its social development."[3] Although *The Broken Fountain* does not pretend to be complete, it does attempt to interpret the behavior of the people it describes in terms of "the surrounding world of wish, whim and thought" that conditions the goals of behavior. Concepts like "the culture of poverty" excuse us from the hard work of unraveling the profound economic and more subtle semiotic relationships that throw an invisible but nonetheless

xix

confining net over the lives and minds of rich and poor alike. Consider for a moment the grease-covered plastic flowers that adorn lower-class kitchens in barrios, ghettos, and *bidonvilles* around the urban world. The poor correctly identify the sign "flowers in the house" with wealth and high status, since, in fact, fresh flowers do adorn the homes of the wealthy and the powerful. Unable to afford the real thing, they settle for the less expensive plastic sign. Their taste in cars, clothing, and furniture often partakes of this yearning to appropriate the power of an elite sign. But the effort is doomed to finish in mockery. Radically torn from its context, the sign will stand on its head and howl.

But there is another conceptual hazard that undermines an urban anthropology of the world's poor. Anthropologists are not only trained in the study of small-scale communities, they are committed to the discovery, description and even to the invention of such forms. In an early review of what is arguably Oscar Lewis' only enduring masterpiece, *The Children of Sanchez*, Eric Wolf situated Lewis' problematical notion of a culture of poverty within "the larger class of cultures that Sapir labeled 'spurious' as opposed to 'genuine.' " In the tightly woven communities of "genuine" cultures, Wolf writes (paraphrasing Sapir) "sociality is productive of symbolic forms that relate the more remote ends to the more immediate ones":

> Yet other societies pit the social actors endlessly against each other in competition for the scarce and irregular resources from which they must derive their livelihood. Then social synchronization produces neither regularity, nor predictability, nor consistency, and every actor must seek his own personal compensations for the defeats suffered at the hands of life. Anthropologists have gloried in the richness of cultures in which great ritual dramas enfold the individual in a mantle of personal and group identity and security;

but their task as recorders of man's various destinies has made them take increasing note of that great plurality of cultures in which the tensions of life are not compensated for by collective dreaming.[4]

Although the preindustrial city may have been capable of generating interactive and symbolic forms that were integrative vertically as well as laterally (consider an institution like Mardi Gras), the industrial and postindustrial cities of the West provide their citizens neither with the residential nor the social nor the ideological continuity that is a prerequisite to the growth of "genuine" culture. Instead of mapping the contours of a living community composed of richly fleshed-out persons, the anthropologist who finds himself adrift in such a landscape becomes at worst a scribbler doing sums and at best a reporter on this or that strategy for the maximization of "personal compensations." In a "spurious" cultural setting where individuals, especially young individuals, are denied access to the sorts of experiences (of love, hope, and fear) that help them to define and defend their humanity, we can predict a range of compensatory styles. We might briefly summarize these as addictive, predatory and protean.

In *Civilization and Its Discontents,* Freud set up a dialectic between addiction and renunciation. In Freudian terms, all culture is, of necessity, rule-governed, representing not so much the hypertrophy of the instincts as their effective renunciation and control. Insofar as a culture based its ethos on premises that induced its members to pursue both pleasure and privacy, it would destroy the sources of its own stability.[5] One might argue that as a capitalist world-culture based solely on a mystique of acquisition successfully erodes those surviving sources of precapitalist value (whether grounded in kinship, religion, ethnicity, or even nationalism), the frequency of addictive and private as opposed to renunciatory and public (responsible) behavior will increase dramatically. The vulnerability of unemployed youth to the global invasion of psychotropic substances, as well as their employment in the drug-distributive sector, is not a mark of their marginality. Rather, they are members of a historical, ultimately suicidal, vanguard.

The predatory style, likewise, issues, not from the periphery, but from the center of our capitalist civilization's dazzling and terrible dynamism. No one, not even Dostoevsky, has penetrated closer to the desires that cling like nodules to the roots of the will to maim and murder better than the American novelist Richard Wright. His anti-hero, Bigger Thomas, kills accidentally, but in killing, and only in comparably drastic acts of violence, can he experience the exalted flush of identity. According to Wright, "All Bigger Thomases, white and black, felt tense, nervous, hysterical and restless." Their personalities did not mature organically from within but were imposed upon them by a "highly geared world whose nature was conflict and action, a world whose limited area and vision imperiously urged men to satisfy their organisms, a world that existed on a plane of animal sensation alone."[6]

The absence of a moral anchorage in enduring communities, the hollowing out of older repositories of value and belief and the futurist celebration of action as a mechanical force that does not, of itself, build anything but merely explodes and destroys the dignity and grace of beings and things are features of an emerging global mass culture that renders all of us, in some sense, snatched and remnant, patched together. But there is yet another bizarre feature of experience in spurious cultures that is exaggerated in the lives of the poor. The pace of change in such cultures, catapulting the individual through a series of unpredictable dislocations in time and space, pressures people to recast their entire mode of relating to the domain of value and belief, leading to a type of personality that Robert Jay Lifton has designated "Protean."

The Protean style has affinities with that archetypal component of personality that Jung subsumed under the mythological category of the Trickster. In preindustrial societies, a range of expressive forms, including sacred clowning and *carnevale*, provided individuals with a sophisticated logic of reversals by which they might counteract the tendencies toward both symbolic and psychic ossification that are side-effects of the formula for "genuine" culture. In the mercantile, two-class societies of the pre-modern Mediterranean, the figure of Trickster underwent first an Odyssean and finally a picaresque metamorphosis into a clever thief. According to Lifton, the postmodern period, with its rapid and successive political and economic upheavals as well as its ability, through media, to retrieve, juxtapose and project (in an instant, anywhere) any culture's repertoire of sacred images, creates a new and more sinister context for the expression of Trickster's shape-shifting imperatives. Unable to remain moored to any set of beliefs for very long, the self retreats into either a "cool" cynicism or else clings, in desperation, to a constrictive fundamentalism:

> Until relatively recently, no more than a single ideological shift was likely to occur in a lifetime, and that one would be long-remembered for its conflict and soul searching. But today it is not unusual for several such shifts to take place within a year or even a month, whether in the realm of politics, religion, aesthetic values, personal relationships, or style of living. Quite rare is the man or woman who has gone through life holding firmly to a single ideological vision. More usual is a tendency toward ideological fragments, bits and pieces of belief systems that allow for shifts, revisions and recombinations.[7]

In Naples, in 1984, it was not uncommon for me to

encounter garbage men and parking lot attendants who were experimenting sequentially and sometimes simultaneously with variants of folk religion, Catholicism, Marxism, Neo-Fascism, Evangelical Protestantism, and even Satanism. Not yet fully literate but no longer versed in the proverbial certitudes of a vanishing oral tradition, these people were, in effect, defenseless against what Edmund Carpenter has referred to as the relentless "phantom blows" that are delivered to all of us daily by the mass media.[8]

Whether, and in what measure, these styles (addictive, predatory, and protean) that we have associated with the category of the spurious come to dominate an individual or a group will be a function of the integrity of preexistent structures of interaction and belief. Following the lead of Herbert Gutman in his study of the adaptive capacities exhibited by black families in slavery, we ask how people in poverty respond to the test of oppression.[9] What means do people have at their disposal for the effective defense of their humanity? Insofar as the needs of growing children are not ignored and repudiated, insofar as the fierce energies of young men are not allowed to dissipate, insofar as families and neighborhoods manage to cohere as units of guardianship and reciprocity and insofar as some possibility of artistic or religious transcendence is mandated in ritual and in the myriad forms of expressive culture, then we might confidently predict the survival of those capacities for both joy and sacrifice that we subsume under the familiar category of the human.

In his by now classic study of concentration camp survivors, Terence Des Pres defined survival as "an experience with a definite structure, neither random nor regressive nor amoral."[10] Against the imperious impulse of the starving to steal from their neighbors, the prisoners enforced a Hobbesian "Bread Law," punishing with death the theft of another's means to live. Against the scarcity of food and medicines, they burglarized the warehouses and smuggled supplies through the most venal and corrupt of the guards. The camps sustained thriving black markets in everything from aspirin to sausage. Prisoner morality was pragmatic, unsentimental, and sly. Generosity was extended only to those who demonstrated the will to resist and live on for another day. Finally, against the Nazi technique of "excremental assault" they countered with a heightened, if only symbolic, concern for the details of personal grooming and cleanliness, even to the point of splashing their faces with the only washwater available, the meager ration of fetid coffee that was distributed in the mornings. Although poor people do not often confront the radical evil represented by the Fascist personality, I think that the relevant parallels between the structure of survival in the camps and among the urban poor of Naples whom I studied in 1974 will be apparent to the reader of *The Broken Fountain*.

In 1984, the people with whom I had worked were facing new challenges. The urban economy upon which they were dependent was changing. Both the municipal and tertiary sectors were expanding. In other words, there were more sinecures and more sweat shops. The earthquake-damaged housing stock of the city center was not being renewed and pressure on urban real estate was increasing from all classes.[11] Anxiety over shelter was at least as intense as the fear of total unemployment. Street markets and bazarres had atrophied. In less than a decade, the presence, sale, and use of drugs had become a ubiquitous feature of life at Fontana del Re and, in fact, meant that my taking up residence again in the same locale was too dangerous to contemplate. Not only were former *picaros* and purse-snatchers armed now and sporadically affluent, but organized crime had moved in to fill the political and entrepreneurial void that had been created by the failure of civic institutions. The family, however, appeared to be holding its own. The petty criminals and coke-dealers at Fontana del Re tended to be responsible husbands and fathers, perhaps because of the enormous sacrifices that their wives were willing to make during their prison terms. In fact, in the family that I worked with closely, conjugal bonds were kept in a good state of repair. Marriages received a continuous infusion of supportive sentiment and (as I discovered through their reactions to my own divorce) strong moral sanctions were invoked against their dissolution. The mother-daughter dyad proved to be especially durable and provided an axis along which services and resources could be transferred.[12]

The epilogue that adds to this edition does not attempt to cover, in any explicit or didactic way, all of these critical issues. In the manner of the first edition, I have constructed a narrative of one anthropological pilgrim's halting progress. But whereas in 1974, the image of the ruined fountain provided a metaphor by which I might pass from analysis to understanding, in 1984, it was the figure of Ribera's laughing crippled beggar that gave me the courage to tell the tale and heal.

The Broken Fountain

Paean to the City

Journal entry, 5/17/75,
last day in Naples

I embraced my friends. . . . As I left to board, the
morning sun was bright to blinding. The plane
thrust upward, lifting and careening, dipping
past the stark crater, and the receding sea-
mountains, sunken in their dense silvery
mists—on to the green plain, on to
Rome, to New York, to future . . .

I ARRIVED IN Naples on a cold, wet, abysmally gray day of early April. I was frightened and apprehensive. I didn't speak more than a few sentences of Italian, and I was geographically lost. As I followed the crowds from the railroad station up what seemed to be the main boulevard, looking for a hotel, I stole glances into the side streets. The boulevard was modern and bustling, lined with drab turn-of-the-century office and residential buildings. But the side streets, the narrow, winding *vicoli*, appeared shadowy and broken, far older in architecture and somehow removed from the activity of the main street.

I soon stopped at an inexpensive hotel, grayer than the day itself but near what seemed to be a large working-class zone. I checked in, and after a few minutes of rest in the dull room, I ventured into the old quarter for my first confrontation with the world I had come to study and know.

1

The darkening streets echoed with the wailing of car horns and phonographs and babies. They were hung with strings of lights and had been built to human, not mechanical, proportions. The small Italian cars were slowed down, pinned and trapped between groups of people, blocked by other cars, or otherwise frustrated in their movement. But there was a rush of humanity, teeming inward and outward from the buildings, flowing through the streets, collecting and pausing in the open spaces that were markets.

Girls walked by me, swaying and chattering, arm in arm, and pairs of young men strutted past close behind them. They also walked arm in arm. Boys shouted and darted in and out of doorways, while mothers hurried about everywhere, clutching at the hands and elbows of their offspring, who in turn held on to their straying younger siblings, in haphazard chainlike formations. And in the midst of this whirl of noise and voices and streaming, rain-muted colors, a boy on a motorbike zoomed up and down, savoring the joy of speed and caring as little for the lives of others as for his own.

The adobe-colored buildings leaned about me like low ravines. They were all festooned with laundry. Some had small, arched entranceways and deep-set windows. Others were more regal in aspect, with great iron-filigreed portals. In all of the edifices there were the same ground-floor cavelike dwellings, the famous *bassi*. In one of these little homes, which seemed cozy and warm to me, at least five small children were bouncing up and down on the large matrimonial bed, like little clowns on a trampoline.

As I walked I unconsciously stopped and looked at the scenes that drew my attention. People stared back and probably realized I was a foreigner by my clothes. The looks of the old women frightened me. They were the sentinels of that world, on guard for intruders. They sat about in the street on chairs and stools, and peered from doorways. Their faces were hard and embittered and drawn toward the mouth. They looked me over, up and down, as if to ask why I was there and why I would not go away. The faces of the young women were becoming like those of the old. Like the old, many were dressed in black, while by contrast their men were clad in the brightest of colors, stretched tight around the frame.

Stalls were everywhere, selling dry goods and cigarettes, bread, cheese, oil, wine, olives, and vegetables—all of it spilling out onto the cobblestones. The air was faintly scented with the odor of scallions. The colors were riotous. The fish displays impressed me as neat abstractions of black and white and silver. There were rows of white squid and bushels of sleek eels, and stacks of a long flat fish, like cut pieces of silver ribbon. I remember the delicate feet of the clams, the color of pure coral, waving back and forth in their large wooden buckets.

In the days that followed, I wandered through many of the poorer districts of Naples. I made forays into the forbidding labyrinth of dark lanes near the port, as old as the *Decameron* whose tales they inspired. I explored the brighter section called Sanità, which looked as though it were hewn from a hillside of volcanic rock, then bleached by the sun and the rains of five centuries, so that now it gleamed like a crumbling honey-colored hive in the sun. I was approached with pistols for sale in the sinister market section of Forcella, which sells everything that the species is capable of smuggling. Finally there was the zone of my first exploration, the old Spanish quarter, which at night was dominated by the prostitutes, gathered near their fires, and the geisha-like faces of the transvestites.

In those early days I was apprehending only the surfaces of things, but there is much to be learned from sur-

3

faces. From the whole torrent of impressions a hidden figure seemed to be emerging (and receding as fast), a
formal if loose arrangement of select qualities and contradictions. In the donning of a sweater, or the sipping of a
caffè, there was always the same fine, brisk grace of movement, the same high sense of style. Etiquettes in all domains of behavior were elaborate and subtle, but people
were comfortable with their bodies in Naples in ways that
would scandalize an American.

What could be more typical of Naples than the occasional lavender veil of wisteria, softening some cen-
turies-old façade? But even the most drab concrete apartment houses, stained with a wash of fading yellow paint
and patched with the jagged blue fiberglass of their broken terraces—even these bunkerlike structures were rendered aesthetically unique by the arrangement of cement
and metal and plastic, and the dozen or so flowerpots
enlivening every balcony. Everywhere there seemed to be
the same valleylike topography to the street scenes in the
overflow of humanity and stall-produce, whether the walls
were made out of homogenized orange fire-brick or gracious, crumbling, pink terra-cotta. Houses and pastry alike
were decorated with the same colors, because life in
Naples is an event to be celebrated, because existence is a
movable, continuing feast.

I came to know the city better in the faces of its people, in their bearing, and in the flow of their speech. Faces
were unmasked to me in Naples, fragile or tough, young,
or else old, smooth or rough, with no room for middle or
blurring categories. Returning to me always were the looks
of the old women, hunched and suspecting, with their
black steeled eyes glistening with hostility and warning.
The sore of poverty was upon Naples, and the marks of
age. Broken things littered all the streets of the old quarters, broken doors and furniture, broken walls, broken

4

bicycles and toys. Everywhere I looked, bent, twisted old people moved painfully up the narrow, climbing lanes. Some moved in slow, throbbing, rhythms, and some with light, comically distorted motions. Some moved with bowed somber dignity, and some moved with the birdlike grace of children.

The language of the poor was expressed in shout and song as much as in ordinary talk, and seemed different from the conversational flow I was picking up in restaurants and bars. In effect there are two languages in Naples; and Italian, for the lower classes—if it is spoken at all—takes a low second place to the Neapolitan dialect. One day I went to the rocks by the port to get some sun. All around me there were groups of boys, of all ages, scattered in pairs and clusters. They were stretched out over the rough scorched rocks or diving into the cold blue water, shouting and calling to one another in the elusive, and to me, totally secret language of the dialect. If Italian, as I was learning it, seemed studied and clear and, in its crystalline grace, evocative of feminine beauty, Neapolitan struck me as primitive and flowing and masculine. In Neapolitan the voice is thick and husky and low. It makes women sound mannish. It streams outward, rough and fast, a veritable rapids of speech. Playing within it is a music, a faraway, languorous water music. In even the simplest cry and certainly the commonest, the oft-repeated "Guagliu', vien' 'a ccà" (Boy, come here), there is a complex orchestration of jubilation and longing and grief. For the call begins with an impulsive glad outburst of sound. It falls midway into a plea. It fades and dies in a low grieving moan. I realized intuitively that day, as I was to learn later, how the dialect as an exotic language enhances the fact of community, closing off outsiders. At the same time, it reaffirms, in its exuberant, rising crescendos, the imperative of sociality, while brooding, in its wearied, almost agonized descents, on the inevitable dilemmas of individual isolation.

The poor boys of Naples are the living symbols of its history and the carriers of its traditions, much as altar boys intermediate the flow of grace from deity to worshipper. In the elegant park by the sea, the Villa Comunale, they arrange themselves in circles on the sun-beaten green to play soccer or cards. They jump wantonly into the fountains; they strip naked, comparing and experimenting, heads tossing, their feet dancing as if on hot coals. In the luxuriant late-afternoon haze, a balloon-man floats by like an image from a dream. Wealthy women stroll, serene-faced, with their maids and baby-carriages, like Parisian matrons in a painting by Seurat. All are oblivious to the boys. It is part of divine order that all should be as they are, and it is left to the boys to protect the integrity of the scene. So to my foreigner's intrusive glance, one young fellow, wet and shivering, looked up at me and laughed and shook his penis furiously, imploring me to come closer for a better look—his companions around him doubling over the jets of water, hopping with glee!

The pulsation of life impressed itself upon me in Naples as it has nowhere else, and not only in the teeming, romantic quarters. I recall walking, a few days after arrival, through the blighted periphery of the city—a confusion of gas stations and junkyards, warehouses and new and old apartment buildings. I came upon a large vacant lot, dusty and barren, circumscribed and enclosed as if it were a prison yard by a disintegrating wall of broken tenements. I noticed some children playing in a corner, when suddenly, appearing as if out of nowhere, a small carnival was in process of setting itself up, a clatter of poles and bells. And no sooner was one ride up, a small, circling ramshackle swing, than it was rushed into operation before any of the others could be assembled. As the children

6

clambered on, their mothers gathered around, laughing and cheering for this diminutive spectacle, in one suddenly animate corner in that barren desert of a place, with the whitish sky above, and the strewn tires and the dust, and the crushed and shattered fragments of glass, like salt, below.

The spirit of place in Naples is the living force of the place. It is resolute and passionate, but it is also unconscious, and insensate to the prod of awareness and reason. As such it can enrage, or it becomes hypnotic. The movement in Naples—the traffic jams, the pushy, shoving crowds, the absence of lines forming for anything, the endless barrage of shouts falling like arrows on the ears, the simultaneous clash of a million destinations and petty opposed intentions—combine into a devastating assault on the senses. Or else the entire scene retreats, slowing and setting finally into a brilliantly colored frieze depicting a grand, if raucous, *Commedia*. One could pass a lifetime just watching the show and contemplating; and pass away into one's own contemplations. The tendency of the soul in Naples is toward forgetfulness, to let consciousness fall into abandon, into the simpler mode of unexamined living. But perhaps it was only the yearning of my inner self, removed from the pressures of past and future. How often I wanted to lose myself in Naples, in the endless procession of light tones passing, in the sunsets of rose gold with their light pressed from roses; the city at dusk, set like a fading ivory reliquary, beneath Vesuvius on the sea.

chapter two

Fieldwork in Naples

Journal entry, 7/20/74

. . . they don't let you be. The self has to fight
for survival here, or it strangles in the grip of
a hundred stronger wills. How I hate them!

IN THE BEGINNING, the world of the Neapolitan poor seemed impenetrable to me. The whole society seemed impenetrable, but the world of the poor was especially private and self-contained. In my walks through the lower-class districts, I was an unobtrusive observer, a receiver of impressions quietly passing through. But I always felt like an unwelcome intruder and made no attempt to settle in alone. I knew that I would have to find someone from within to serve as a diplomatic intermediary, someone who could introduce me and explain me and reassure people, in their own language, that my intentions were honest.

Ordinary people going about the business of their daily lives aren't likely to have time for disoriented anthropologists. Strangers far from home tend to encounter strangers closer to home, a kind of meeting of lonely with estranged minds. Since the exogenous stranger is, very often, in his home environment, one of the "endogenous estranged," the chances for anthropologists and expatriates to make native friends abroad are probably related to the degree of alienation present in the host society. I had cause for optimism.

At first I thought I would find my salvation in a young man (whom I met in a trattoria), with a lean, hawklike look, who told me he was a disillusioned Communist intellectual and promised to help me settle in a poor zone. Giorgio impressed me in his contradictions. His intelligence was keen and incisive but his chronic boredom was depressing to me, and I often had the uncomfortable impression that my main function with him was to provide relief from *tedium vitae*, a social disease among the allowanced sons of the southern Italian middle classes. Giorgio was intensely concerned with political matters, but he had lost his young man's will to have a political impact on the world through either politics or sociology. When I last spoke to him, he was impressing himself into the service of a wealthy industrialist as a kind of general factotum.

Giorgio's English improved over the month we spent chatting together, and I became familiar with middle-class Naples, but to my exasperation he evinced little enthusiasm for the real issue at hand, which for me was establishing myself in my research. He was simply unwilling to mingle with lower-class people in any way. But if he was hesitant to rub shoulders with the poor in an intensely class-divided society, he did want to help me as he could, and introduced me to a great number of people, mostly students and professionals. Through him I met my major field assistant and partner, who became, for the duration of my stay in Naples, my blessing and my curse, my sternest teacher and one of my dearest friends.

Carlo was like Giorgio in many ways. I suppose that was why they didn't get along; each of them mirrored too well the societal irresponsibilities of the other. (Both were in their late twenties, living on parental money, and neither had completed his university degree.) But if Giorgio was lean like a bird of prey, Carlo was massive like a bull.

10

His size and sheer bulk were menacing, but he laughed at himself often, like a rotund medieval friar. One easily laughed with him.

Carlo was almost as interested in my research as I was. He offered concrete help immediately. He was broadly educated, well-read, and politically sophisticated, but never far from his roots in rocky Lucania. He was ribald and coarse and totally at home in the Neapolitan dialect. He had friends in one of the largest lower-class zones, and wasted no time introducing me and explaining my research intentions to them.

But despite Carlo's introductions, my first attempt to make entry in a Neapolitan poor district failed. Although I succeeded in making friends with three young working-men and became quite a celebrity at their nightly hangout, I attracted the attention of other people in the neighborhood who decided that my anthropologist pose was a clever disguise. I had to be a police agent or a spy of some sort. There was enough illegal activity going on to make people afraid of me. My new friends were criticized for associating with me, and I was threatened with beating if I persisted in my attempt to live in the area. At the height of the suspicion, when I would arrive nightly at the local bar, my new acquaintances used to sit me down for a caffè and fire questions at me, meticulously interviewing me as to my whereabouts during the preceding twenty-four hours and, it seemed to me, the preceding twenty-four years. My answers only confirmed their worst opinion of me.

"Nice try, Tommaso; you're a smart operator. If we weren't Neapolitans, you'd have fooled us easy." The bartender spoke his slowest, clearest Italian for me, conjuring visions of my skeleton dissolving in a lime vat. Everyone laughed heartily. But Neapolitans always convey unpleasant truths via jokes. I congratulated them all on their peculiarly Neapolitan astuteness and agreed that it would be better for all of us if I limited my fieldwork in their area to an occasional caffè and game of cards.

Both Carlo and I were surprised at my rejection. But we were also struck by the powerful, defensive sense of community which my stranger's threat had incited—the rapidity of closure in the face of danger, and the refusal to risk and suffer the presence of anyone from the outside who could not be easily accounted for. I was discouraged, but I respected these people for their caution. I thought they must have learned some painful lessons from history.

I was therefore surprised soon afterward when I managed to settle into one of the most infamous corners of Naples, notorious as a foul-smelling den of thieves and whores. I had been walking one night with Carlo, and he showed me the area on a whim, a kind of enclosed, plebian compound, dating from the seventeenth century. Neither of us expected to discover that an apartment was available, a damp little grotto of a place with low, arched, curving walls and a balcony looking down onto the street space and courtyard below. Carlo introduced me as his student-cousin, come from America to study local customs on a scholarship. I agreed to pay the somewhat exorbitant rent. When I signed the lease the next afternoon, I was sure that the landlord, a shrewd local shopkeeper, thought me stupidly naive to commit myself to live in a place like *Fontana del Re*, so named for the battered remains of a fountain carved into one of the corners. He warned me in somber, paternal tones not to speak to anyone. But no sooner had I finished signing than a young fellow in his late teens leaped up into my room, bounding over the balcony railing, to find out who I was and what I wanted. He playfully pickpocketed my wallet, and upon finding very little money inside, remarked disparagingly that he was in better shape than I, having brought off three successful bag-snatchings the day before. I was

12

amazed at his honesty and trust. I asked him his name. "Pepe the Top" he replied, and as he said so, he tilted and twirled about on his toes like a ballet dancer. His face was blackened with dirt and he looked like a devil, come up from Dante's *Inferno*. I knew I had a friend in him. His eyes gleamed with a glad, protective warmth.

First Day

I moved into my little cell in Fontana del Re the following week. One entered the compound through a wide, crumbling portal. A narrow lane, or *vicoletto*, cut through the structure, leading finally to some ancient steps which emerged onto a small piazza. The clouded light of that warm afternoon seemed darker and denser in the enclosed space beyond the portal. For the first time I saw how littered and broken it actually was. A cacophony of noises, of hammers and shouts, retreated into a whir in my ears, becoming almost a silence, blending with the stagnant, dying light and the heavy, accumulating air.

All the faces in all of the windows, from first floor to sixth, stared down at me intently. People murmured, from balcony to balcony, "l'americano, l'americano." Their looks were questioning and puzzled, but not hostile. Perhaps here there was less to lose by the presence of a stranger, or perhaps they were confident of the severity of their punishment should I prove to be false. Certainly the profit-motivated patronage of my landlord, and the proffered friendship of young Pepe, as well as my purported kin bond with Carlo had combined to neutralize the worst suspicions.

As I walked toward my apartment, with Carlo at my side, I became aware of a commotion behind us. The space of the courtyard flooded with the sounds of the Neapolitan language. A small crowd had gathered in front of an old woman, standing in a second-floor balcony. An old man from a window above, his skin furrowed and brown, caught my eye and began to shout at me his version of what was going on. One of his eyes was pure white, tinged with blue, frozen and unmoving. The other eye darted about as if it were dancing a pantomime, vividly displaying every nuance of his changing meanings. I understood nothing.

The old woman beneath whom the crowd had gathered was heavy and bowed, with white thinning hair and a soiled apronlike garment. Her face was fat and large, with deep fissures and crevices for wrinkles, and massive, jowled cheeks. Her eyes told of her plight. They were limpid and tender, infected, and wet with pain, and floated in the terrible red pools which were her sockets. Her arms were outstretched to the noisy arguing crowd below in a proclamation of helplessness. One arm was crudely bandaged with a filthy cloth. She trembled like a shivering animal. An ambulance arrived. The attendants led her down the stairway. They put her inside the vehicle and drove away.

Her balcony window remained open. A torn black sweater was cast aside on a broken stool, and a tattered piece of nylon had been nailed to the frame as a curtain. I approached closer, but young Pepe pulled me back, warning me of the smell which issued from her room. The small crowd dispersed as people returned to their daily labors. Then I was told why the old woman's arm had been bandaged up. Her arm had been bitten by the rats, they said, which infested her squalid room. She would never be back. They knew it as a certainty. Some were glad to see her go, referring to the stench hanging about her room. And there was talk of blocking up her windows to seal in the rats, and the smell.

14

This was what happened on my first day at *Fontana del Re*. That night, alone and apprehensive in my strange new home, I thought about her wretched end, and wondered about her life, and tried in vain to know, what awful conspiracy of forces had led the infant to this.

Getting to Know Fontana del Re

My first visitors at Fontana del Re were the children, who came knocking at my door every morning, shy and curious, asking for small change. They huddled before me in small congregations, effervescent with laughter, their dirt-blackened hands outstretched and quivering with anticipation. I saw them as I had always seen children. Each, in his or her nascent individuality, expressed a unique human possibility, springing from the natural play of selfishness and innocence and growth. But as I came to know them better in the months that followed, I saw them differently. They looked older than children, and some of their faces were already pulled with the lines of years to come, so that one knew how they would look when they were very old. In their actions they were like lit fuses, or firecrackers going off, in snapping little bursts of violence. Whenever I let them into my apartment, they threw themselves wrestling onto the bed. They took pens from the desk and jabbed at each other furiously, escalating their play into pummeling and tears. They charged at me with the pens, poking at my sides, and giggled about the sexual indiscretions of their older brothers and sisters.

The children came every morning and sporadically during the day. When I pretended to be out, they would chant my name and hammer against my door. I would rise and answer, and see them and not see them, bright and trembling little forms, yelping in the air about me. When I

15

refused to admit them, they would shake and yelp all the louder, grabbing at my hands and arms and legs, with their excited fingers, until I sent them away, and like so many rabbits they scattered down the crumbling steps into their frenzied play.

Although most of the people who lived there worked for a living, Fontana del Re was justly notorious as a den of thieves. Thievery as a mode of acquisition was especially suited to young men, demanding agility in climbing and speed in flight. The labyrinthine lanes and abandoned apartments provided excellent refuge to the pursued bag-snatcher or car-burglar, and one of the first things my young friend Pepe told me was that if I ever saw him running into the compound never to call out his name. Most of the thieves were in their teens and early twenties. They had a great deal of leisure time and visited me constantly. My apartment became a kind of social club, for caffè drinking and arm-wrestling. Unlike the children, the thieves did not knock. Most followed Pepe's first example and leaped over my balcony. They could enter my room so quietly that I often went on writing for a quarter of an hour before I realized that someone was sitting on the bed behind me, calmly watching me work. Since formal interviews would have read like dossiers, I simply chatted with my new friends. Sometimes I went swimming or fishing with them. But a fishing expedition could easily change its character if there were better catches to be had in the cars parked near the shore. I found myself in several compromising situations.

Among the thieves whom I came to know, one man differed in character and intelligence from the rest. His name was Lorenzo. People always referred to his combined qualities of cunning and generosity. He came to see me one night soon after I had settled in, and began the conversation by telling me about local incidents in which unruly American sailors had been beaten or killed by offended Neapolitans. As he spoke, his eyes were evasive and menacing. His face was handsome and angular, with thick, sharply drawn eyebrows, incising a defiant line across his forehead. After I told him of my hopes to observe and portray his world, he warmed up toward me and offered his help. Since he was illiterate, I would translate into the written word his insights and reflections concerning street life. I was moved by his offer of aid and considered myself fortunate to have won the assistance of a man cast in the mold of the traditional bandit-hero.

But whenever Lorenzo came to see me again, it was to ask if I could write letters or hide stolen merchandise. A week after our initial meeting, I was called from my apartment into the courtyard below. Lorenzo was arguing with a middle-aged Moroccan businessman who spoke some English but no Italian. I was asked to translate. The man had come to Fontana del Re to recover his camera, which he said had been stolen nearby. Lorenzo claimed to know nothing of the camera and told the man to go away. The Moroccan threatened to go to the police. I hesitated to translate but he insisted. I complied. Lorenzo responded by placing his hand on the man's shoulder, as if to open a more friendly line of discourse. Then his free hand gripped the other shoulder, and his head came down into the man's face like a blunt hatchet. The Moroccan fell to his knees. As he lifted his head a kick to the chin sent him reeling backward. Lorenzo fell upon him and jabbed his fist repeatedly into the turned escaping face. People gathered round. The young were excited. But the old women were annoyed by the commotion and called Lorenzo off the man, who seized the opportunity to hobble away on his hands and feet.

The volatility and brute force of Lorenzo's action repelled me, as did the admiration which the other young men subsequently bestowed upon him. Violence was endemic to all the lives which touched mine at Fontana del Re. The weak suffered at the hands of the strong, and took their place as the strong with others still weaker than they.

As the summer drew to a close, I became weary of my association with the young thieves. Although my capacity to speak and understand their language improved, I fell into silences with them and was left to myself. Gradually we became strangers again, and our strangeness was edged with a mutual, unspoken sense of betrayal. I wondered how I might gain access to the other lives I was glimpsing—the lives of the working people, and the interior life of the family. But I pursued no one. I sat at my desk and stared out across the balcony, marking my hours and days by the changing schedule of sounds and colors which were the measures of time at Fontana del Re.

The first sounds of the day at Fontana del Re come from the pigeons stirring in their roosts. Soon after, buckets of water splash onto the cobblestones. Shutters and balconies open. Children begin to cry; fathers begin to shout. The swanlike voice of a young woman glides upward and past. Arguments break out between the housewives on the street, and the roar of their gruff shouting momentarily drowns out all other sound. The traffic noises start and mix with the hammering of the junkmen. Carts rattle into the lane, and baskets are hurriedly lowered from windows as the vendors of fish and vegetables arrive and let forth with their loud vibrato songs. By noon some of the young thieves have wakened, and their phonographs blare out a melange of American rock and Neapolitan folk music. The afternoon is quiet, save for the sporadic squabbling of children and the raised cocksure voices of the little boys. More vendors arrive. An old man hobbles by, hawking long bright wooden poles, newly chipped and flayed, for hanging laundry. The broom-seller passes. He looks like a clumsy tropical bird, with his burden of brilliant turquoise buckets and pink and yellow plastic brooms. Dusk is signaled by the urgent whistle of the milkman and the sirenlike shouts of the mothers, calling their children home.

At night after the supper hour, Fontana del Re is relatively quiet and subdued. In every dwelling, every small overcrowded *basso,* there is the echo and glow of the television. The viewers seem content and relaxed, the old, the young, the families gathered and spread across the few chairs and the large beds that dominate the rooms. Occasionally a motorcycle speeds past. From the high corners and from behind the counters of the locked stores, the enshrined Madonnas watch and listen. She is framed everywhere in a mantle of neon blue. Her light is cool and soft and electric. Her gaze is frozen and mute.

Directly below my apartment was a small junk depository. If the previous day's collections had been good, the noise of washing machines and water heaters being disassembled provided the major accompaniment to my mornings. The depository was owned by a local workman named Stefano. He would do the heavy work of smashing and breaking, helped by his oldest boy. His wife and five smaller children would then crouch around the broken hulk of machinery, as if it were a carcass, to receive and sort the various parts.

One afternoon in late August (perhaps because I had recently bandaged the bruised foot of one of his sons), Stefano invited me to go to the beach with his family and the children of a friend. Climbing into the back of his small truck, I found myself in the midst of a dozen swarming children, who scrambled over me and fought for seating space on my shoulders and knees. The truck rattled and choked its way in a roundabout route through all of Naples until we arrived at an uncrowded shore.

19

Fieldwork in Naples

The beach was a dirty affair, strewn with trash and broken bottles. But the surface of the water was like a roll of silk, blue and unfurling. Tall chalk cliffs and a promontory of pine forest reached into the sea, and in the distance the isle of Capri skimmed the horizon, like a diaphanous silver fin. But turning around and facing away from the ocean, one saw first a row of deteriorating beach cottages, and behind them a massive industrial complex, a snarl of smokestacks and piping, spreading over the low hills.

As soon as we arrived, the children rushed into the water. Stefano's wife, Elena, spread a large blanket and began to unpack the baskets of food. She held an enormous loaf of bread to her neck, as if it were a violin, and deftly sliced it into thick, even pieces. Stefano sat back on a broken beach chair, which leaned sideways into the sand. He looked like a tired old chieftain. He was a short, lean man, with an incongruous paunch and a bony unshaven face. He kept a large cask of wine at his side and refilled my glass as fast as I emptied it; "Drink the nectar, Tommaso, it'll do you good." As we drank he told me about each of his children, pointing them out to me in the water, taking pride in this one, expressing doubt about another, and declaring his love for them all. He described his junk-collecting work and proudly showed me his calluses, the small pointed one on the top of his head, and the other, a smooth egg-sized bump, set between his shoulders.

After a swim we came back to the blanket, which was covered with plates brimming with macaroni, and bowls filled with cutlets, and fried peppers, and piles of bright boiled greens sprinkled with lemon and chopped garlic. Stefano beamed at the food, and then at me; "Pranzo di faticatore" (a workman's lunch), he exclaimed. His wife, a stout woman with a serious, almost grim expression, pre-

20

sided over the serving. The children were silent as she made up the plates. "Am I a good divider, or not, Tommaso?" She bellowed the question at me, allowing the hint of a smile to escape from the corners of her mouth. She took obvious pride in her skill as a cook and in her status as the source and arbiter of who ate what, and when.

The afternoon wore on lazily into dusk, with the sunset gradually deepening into a dense rose-colored haze, saturating every shadow. Stefano played some Neapolitan love songs on a battered tape-recorder, and he and his sons sang along with their favorites, more than compensating for the inaudible portions of the scratchy tape. Stefano's fifteen-year-old son, Ciro, momentarily forgot his customary self-consciousness and sang out in a hoarse loud monotone. When the others jeered at him, he attacked a younger brother, setting off a minor brawl. His mother rose from the blanket, screaming and cursing, and the fighting children scattered in terror. She chased Ciro across the sand, howling after him. Unable to catch him, she flung an empty beer bottle full-force against his back. Ciro collapsed to the sand in tears, but his sobs were for the original tauntings and not his mother's rage. Everyone rushed to his side. His father embraced him, while his mother stroked his hair, and his brothers and little sister clustered round, apologizing and half-teasing him until they elicited a smile.

In the ensuing months, as I became a regular visitor to Stefano's household, I often witnessed similar scenes of explosive violence, followed by some kind of restorative gesture. At their roisterous dinner table, Stefano and the members of his family would give voice to and dramatize the conflicts and tensions of their interlocked lives. Their shabby dining–living room trembled and quaked daily with the shocks of violence and pain which seemed to be, for all the people I knew at Fontana del Re, half of the barter of friendship and love.

Stefano's children lived in fear of the youngest boy and family favorite, the five-year-old Robertino. If, during supper, an older brother became too involved with a plate of macaroni, Robertino would sneak up from behind and beat the startled sibling over the head with a broomstick. As the victim fell from his chair, whimpering, Stefano and the others would chuckle and agree: "Chill' è troppo esagerato, il nostro Robertino!" (He's really too much, isn't he, our Robertino!). But sometimes little Rob would rouse Stefano himself to rage, and then he would chase the boy, like the villain in a silent movie, tripping over chairs and stubbing his toes, as the child scrambled to the safety of a high cupboard, to taunt his father with some choice slang.

Sometimes, if a family quarrel were especially brutal, I found myself trembling and speechless, but my attempts to judge, in a moral sense, were invariably foiled. In moments of excessive wrath, the Signora would take to throwing knives and forks at the offending child. On one of these occasions (since I was seated next to the target) I ducked under the table, whereupon she interrupted her outburst to shout to the others, "Guardate, Tommaso ha paura" (Look, Tommaso is scared). Everyone broke into uproarious laughter as I poked my head up from the folds of the tablecloth to see if it were safe.

Once, when I tried to avoid them for a few days, Stefano and his wife assumed I was homesick. Returning from a shopping foray in the country, they stopped by my apartment to show me their bouquet of fresh basil. As I savored the fragrance of the new herbs, they tried to console me and poured me a glass of dark peasant wine, still bitter with the tannin of the vine.

At first, Stefano's three-room apartment struck me as

ugly and cluttered. An intricate floral wallpaper, yellowed with age, and a motley arrangement of fading prints and garish oil paintings decorated the cracked plaster walls. An elaborate mahogany dresser and sideboard were covered with tawdry figurines and vases and family photographs. Above the entrance to the dining room, two shiny red plates, painted around the edge in a bright gold enamel, were set up like family insignias, and whenever Stefano led me to his table, he pointed up to them with pride: "Sono reale, Tommas'!" (They're royal, Tom!).

As I spent more time with Stefano and his family, I came to appreciate the special qualities adhering to the things which formed an integral part of his home. Whether it was a torn picture of an Egyptian pharaoh or a dime-store painting of Vesuvius, an empty place on the wall had been filled and something pleasing, or at least stimulating to the senses, had replaced a nothingness.

For all the strife in Stefano's household, some things seemed to be protected by an invisible shield. The fish-bowl, with its slender contented goldfish, was always in its same place next to the old radio, and the kitchen Madonna, set in a lacquered shell canopy fashioned by Stefano himself, glowed serene and childlike in her sea-shrine. A wooden birdcage was perched up high, and when the birds sang, Stefano would call for silence, to note their song. A marble stand, found on the street, occupied a place of honor in the living room, to hold co-godfather Carmine's gift of paper flowers. Although these things were simple and common, to Stefano and his family they were the things of life. In a world that was chaotic and noisy and often drab, they were fixed and silent and beautiful. A photograph of John XXIII, or of President Kennedy, meant more than the memory of a particular man, but symbolized their desire to believe in man's capacity for a greatness which was pure. A miniature Statue of Liberty or a stock Baroque figurine told of worlds beyond the frontiers of poverty and class, where tedium and insecurity supposedly did not exist.

Adjacent to Stefano's apartment was a large enclosed porch with a small bedroom attached. During the winter, rainwater collected in a puddle on the shaded patio and never seemed to dry, so that the enclosure gave off an unpleasant odor and attracted a great number of flies and mosquitoes. An old widow lived there with her invalid brother-in-law. She was dwarfed and bent, with a waxy wrinkled face and active clear-blue eyes. I saw her every day on the corner of a major avenue selling wilted flowers from a tin bucket. Sometimes Elena would ask her in for a caffè, and if I were present, she would tease the old lady about the possibilities of a romance with the young American. The old woman never demurred, but entertained everyone by placing her hands on my hips and swiveling her pelvis.

One evening toward the end of winter, I was having supper with Stefano when we heard shouts coming from the widow's apartment. I entered the dark room with Stefano and Elena and their three smallest children. The children giggled. A bare light bulb revealed the sallow, gaunt face of an old man. He was wearing long brown underwear and sat up on a large bed. He pointed to a smaller bed nearby, where the old lady was stretched out. She was fully clothed in three overlapping sweaters and a woolly maroon skirt. Her hands were clenched inside two soiled grey mittens and her blue eyes were wide open, fixed toward the ceiling. Her body was jerking and she was gasping for air. I assumed she was about to die, as did Stefano, who rushed off to telephone her relatives. But Signora Elena sat beside her and scolded her for drinking too much wine. Hoping to soothe her, I tried to stroke her forehead but the old woman pushed my hand away. Meanwhile the children had found some sticks and began to chase one another around the room. Little Rob had a toy pistol, and the firing caps alternated with the old woman's wheezing. A small black dog emerged from beneath the bed. One sharp ear pointed upward; the other appeared eaten and rotten, half torn away. The children teased the animal with their sticks. The dog snapped and growled, and curled back as if to strike, and then began to growl again. Signora Elena laughed at the havoc of the scene, but I shrunk back, feeling alien and cold in that damp, squalid place. The chaos of noise swirling about me hushed in my ears, and all I heard was the mean low whining of that crazed little animal. Soon the old widow closed her eyes, and her breathing became regular as she fell into a deep sleep. The next morning she was at her usual post selling flowers.

People weren't always solemn about suffering and death at Fontana del Re. It depended on who suffered and who died. But if death made a noise in an old woman's room, it was a common enough sound, easily drowned out by the din and racket of life.

Being on the bottom of society involves a continual struggle with the grimness of that fact. The people I knew at Fontana del Re were existential fighters. They often fought outside the rules and they always got hurt. It is the poor who must express, in idioms of violence and sentimentalism, the fragility of most social identities and bonds. It is they who must somehow survive, and go on, and extract satisfaction from life at the bottom of the well of loneliness and boredom which contains and threatens to dampen so much of human consciousness.

When I went to Naples, I thought that poor people would be more noble for their poverty, and I thought that the life of a man who troubled to enter into some empathetic relation with lives so ennobled would become more noble as well. But the realities of lower-class life in Naples are not ennobling, neither to participants nor observers.

chapter three

The Neapolitan Personal Style

Journal entry, notes on a festa, 9/19/75

*The singer? She was sassy, with a green silk dress
and gold sequins. She belted her songs, real
sentimental, but full of plot, so the people
nearly wept as they sang with her.*

WHEN I FLED Naples, I fled like a sleepwalker, brooding, silent, and alone. I fled to Rome and to Florence, but no sooner would I be off the train and checking into a hotel than I would feel a dull, metallic edge cooling in my chest, becoming colder and sharper within me as the days of walking and viewing went by. Then I had to restrain myself from returning straightaway. Then Naples, which had been my prison, appeared on the horizon of my consciousness as a city of hope.

After one such flight and impulsive return, on a withering hot afternoon in late summer, I stood at the portals of Fontana del Re, hesitating to enter. The odor of the sewer reared in the air above me like a spirit conjured up from below. The rubble of a fallen palazzo fumed nearby with powder and dust. From a far balcony a curse was cast out like a stone. But then I heard my name, loud above me, being hurled against the walls. In a moment, Pepe was running toward me, grinning wildly, with his arms outstretched. He leaped upon me, toppling the two of us, and he embraced me violently, punching me and wanting to know why I had gone away without telling him.

The place of affliction and the city of hope: in terms of this polarity I was constrained to understand Naples. The place of ashes and blood, the place of flowers and wine—a city of greetings and concealed knives: these were the harsh dialectics of a people's life.

One day I went to Capri. At the end of the day an enormous crowd had gathered to board the ferry. There are many ferries back to Naples. I had chosen the cheapest. As the ferry backed into the dock and the gates opened, the crowd surged forward. I was lifted off the ground and tossed onto the deck. Afraid of being trampled, I scrambled to a high place and watched the scene unfold below.

The people had jammed the entrance and were more or less stuck there. On the pier beyond was the line, where others waited in patience to board, and in front was the deck, where those who had come through recovered themselves. But in this liminal zone, which was like a whirlpool, people were squirming and wrestling and weaving about as though possessed. Several women were beating a man adjacent to them with their baskets and bags. To no avail, people seized one another and pushed, only to be seized and pushed in turn. For no apparent reason, punches and blows were delivered in secret to the unwary. People moaned and winced and cried out in agony and fear, but there were many who seemed to relish this opportunity for savagery. Once in the maelstrom, they accepted the terms of the maelstrom and were transformed by it until, as if by magic, they found themselves on board, disheveled and shaken. I watched them with revulsion.

But within ten minutes, on the upper deck the Neapolitans had found one another. They called to each other, to share food and wine. They formed themselves into circles of laughter and song. Some boys from the Forcella district set about teasing an old peasant woman from

Bari, mocking her accent, but she got the better of them every time and the deck went uproarious with laughter. Soon Naples came into full view. The people broke their bread together and sang songs and drank more wine. Far off, the cliffs of Capri receded like opals in a mist, and a cool, brisk wind swept in from the sea.

It is because of their capacity for community and individuality at once that the Neapolitan situation is tragic and not merely pathetic. For they are a people who have perfected the art of *communitas* while at the same time celebrating the human personality for the riches it contains. Could they fashion a utopia of their own, I am certain it would be anti-platonic—a social organization for diversity and maximal self-expression. Just as Plato would have cast out actor and playwright as subversives, the Neapolitans would give these a central role, for they represent the full range of human feelings and catch all the rays that shine from the prism that is man. But the Neapolitans can only rarely utilize their social and dramatic skills in the service of utopia. More often they are caught in the maelstrom, as they were beneath the cliffs of Capri. They retreat into the violence of unbridled emotion, or else they become dissemblers. In the slum's theater of cruelty, they each play their little part of rogue.

Styles of Interaction

Soon after arriving in Naples, I was invited to the home of a dishwasher friend for Easter. When it came time to open a bottle of sparkling wine, my friend went to the balcony and popped the cork. The wine foamed upward, then fell onto the head of an old woman who was sitting on the balcony below. The old woman began to grumble, ominously, and then to shout and finally to thunder. When her fury did not let up, I was sure that the afternoon had been spoiled. But my friend Mimmo and his family were more than amused by the accident; every horrible curse sent them into new fits of laughter. Within five minutes the old woman was seated beside me, sipping the *spumante* she had not been originally invited to taste. She was joking and gossiping, obviously delighted to be a part of the group. Her voice was scratchy and when she laughed she revealed her gums, with their two remaining tusklike teeth.

In Naples, even the most banal events can be elevated to the level of drama. The social exterior of the poor quarters is histrionic. Its tonalities are theatrical. If drama was originally invented as a metaphor for life, in Naples the metaphor has overwhelmed the referent, and society presents itself as a series of plays within plays.

One afternoon, walking along a narrow lane in old Naples, I was startled by the sight of a bent-up Fiat careening toward me. I pressed myself against the nearest wall and winced with terror as the car grazed me and stopped. Driving the car was my friend Pepe from Fontana del Re. When he finally stopped laughing, he insisted that I ride with him. I boarded and we were off on a fearful, reckless joyride. As he raced up and down the curving streets, which were thick with children, Pepe complained to me that people did not respect him. He had robbed some tires and hidden them only to have some older thieves rob them from him in turn. To get his tires back, he had to argue at length and even flash his knife. As he told the story, his anger intensified and reflected in his driving, which was hyper-aggressive and jerky, all short stops and false starts. He went on to denigrate a close friend who had insulted Pepe's brother for having tolerated a slap in the face from a local hoodlum: "I'm going to have to really hurt someone in this quarter. And then they won't take me for a fool. They'll respect me all right. You'll see. Real soon. I'm going to have to really hurt!"

A few days later, returning to my apartment in the evening, I found Pepe waiting at my door. His father had thrown him out into the street. When I invited him in, he paced about the room with clenched fists, cursing his father and threatening revenge. We had some brandy and he sat down. Suddenly his face, which was coarse and dark although still boyish, became softer. Suddenly the anger passed out of it and he covered his eyes with his hands. His shoulders collapsed and his body crumpled and he sobbed bitterly, mumbling over and over, "No one has ever cared about me in my life. No one!" He referred to his mother, who had gone off with another man many years before. Reflecting on this episode, I recalled the words of Gramsci, in one of his *Letters from Prison:*

I've always believed that there is an Italy we don't know about because we never see it and which is quite different from the apparent and visible one. In most civilized countries an abyss separates what you see and what you don't see, but the abyss here is deeper than in any other civilized country. In Italy, the noisy piazze, the enthusiastic shouting, the verboseness and ostentation, all cover over the realities of private life more than anywhere else.[1]

In Naples, behavior was heavy with meaning which could either reveal truth or mask it, and spontaneity and artifice ran into one another like the tints of a watercolor.

I remember vividly one of the tenser moments of my fieldwork, when late one night I was called out into the street by an imposing young tough whom I did not know. It was during a period of friction between myself and the young men of the district over my demands for minimal privacy. Most of these fellows were assembled nearby as "detached" onlookers.

31

The stranger was nervous and high-strung. He accused me of various offenses, the most serious being that I was, in the eyes of the local community, an annoying foreign pest. But despite the gravity of this last accusation, my accuser smiled at me and joked throughout. He put his arm around my shoulder and drew me away from the others, as though he and I were knowledgeable in ways that they were not. At one point, when I smiled at something he said, he went so far as pinch my cheek in a gentle, patronizing way.

When he touched my cheek, breaking the bounds of acceptable physical contact, I realized that the denouement of the episode was at hand. I pretended to be at ease and warned him, half in jest, about the hardness of my head should he contemplate smashing his against it. We began to exchange comments on a more equal footing, matching wits and never breaking eye-contact. I refuted the charges, invoking the bonds of mutual friendship between myself and members of the onlooking jury. The atmosphere lightened, and within a half hour everyone was behaving as though nothing irregular had occurred in the first place.

At Fontana del Re a high value was placed on façades, on what Erving Goffman has called "the maintenance of expressive control." If a man would fear and tremble, he should appear courageous and still. If he would release his hostility toward an enemy, he should remain patient to calculate a silent revenge. Even their humor was remarkably deadpan and straight-faced; the telling of a joke was a playful training session in the suppression of feeling. Action was perceived as a vehicle of communication. In the language of symbolic action, a rage might be a plea and a kiss an economic stratagem. An act of blind violence might be a desperate bid for prestige, and a playful caress on the cheek could presage a savage physical attack.

Although the skillful telling of a joke might call for some suppression of feeling, the reaction to it certainly did not. The people of Fontana del Re readily delivered themselves over to pure feeling when nothing impeded its expression! I remember Pepe's reaction to the predicament of his friend, after he had confused the fellow with some American obscenities, learned from me that morning. His delight was convulsive! He leaped into the air, hitting the ground like a spring, and held his stomach and sides. His whole body seemed caught in a cycle of progressive contortions, tightening and then flying apart, as his hooting and his jeers intensified and renewed.

Reactions to frustration were not different in kind from reactions to joy. Tantrumlike episodes were common among children and adolescents. Soon after the incident with Pepe, I encountered one morning, prostrate on the steps to my apartment, the eleven-year-old daughter of a neighbor. She had always impressed me as a soft, lovely girl, buoyant and cheerful. But here she was, sprawled in the dust, kicking and seething. Her feet jerked about crazily, and when I knelt down to help her, she pushed me away, refusing all aid. Her older brother then appeared and informed me that she was angry at her defeat in a quarrel and that I shouldn't concern myself with her. Later in the year, I witnessed him in the throes of a similar reaction. Eventually I realized that the tantrumlike reactions of the young were inversions of the brutal anger of the old. The gestural symbol of impotent rage in Naples is to feign gnawing at one's arm, but if one had power, one's rage need not go underground. Adult men and women at Fontana del Re told me they were subject to flights of control over their physical selves, which might render them dangerous. Fearful child-beating was common; everybody had scars to exhibit.

The people of Fontana del Re used guile instrumen-

33

tally, as it suited them. But the masks they wore were rarely affixed to their faces. In the poor quarters of Naples, every person becomes a playwright and an actor, seeking to determine and organize the reactions of an audience. But every person is a critic as well, more than ready to demolish the transparent devices and weaker props of his fellows. Thus the blunt and disarming frankness of the Neapolitan! Out of this interplay of dramas and critics, some fundamental understanding emerges. People who are unsophisticated in academic matters become masterful psychologists. They will deal with one another and even attempt to love one another, fully aware of each other's ruses and faults.

Brutality and the Social Philosophy

Poor folk are shackled to the necessities of the world. Bound to the world, they take on its rougher contours and re-enact its cruelties. On hot nights in August, after a certain hour at Fontana del Re, the rats would dare to come up from the sewers. The boys who had stayed up chatting would wait for them at the gutters, ready with their stones. I recall once when three of us kept a still, silent vigil. For me it was a desperate game to extinguish the boredom of the evening, but for them it was a hunt, the stalking of a hated enemy. Soon, protruding out of the gutter, sniffing and cautious, was this hooked, blackened snout and the fat gray body behind it. Our rocks came down on the animal as we chased it and shouted. But the rat, momentarily stunned, skittered about in a frenzy, dodging every stone, until he sped away to disappear into another black hole. My friends were amused. They congratulated the rat: "They are cunning, these rats—they are Neapolitan."

No two men at Fontana del Re were more different from one another than Pasqualino and Lorenzo. Lorenzo was intelligent and widely admired. He cut a figure of cruel, harsh beauty, whereas Pasqualino was clumsy and tattered, the butt of everyone's jokes. On another summer evening, the young men of the district were gathered around Lorenzo, who sat astride his motorcycle as though it were a steed. To distract himself, Lorenzo took to tormenting Pasqualino. He beckoned in a friendly way, and when Pasqualino approached, smiling in his clumsy, slightly embarrassed way, Lorenzo slapped him hard on the back. Pasqualino winced and jumped back, muffling his curses. At first the laughter of the others was uneasy, but when Lorenzo repeated the trick ten minutes later, the hilarity was unrestrained. Even Pasqualino was called upon to laugh, and so he did. When I complained at a later point about Lorenzo's behavior, I was sternly silenced with the proverb-cliché: "The big fish eat the little fish. This is the way it is."

On a wet chilled night in early fall, I was greeted at my door by four young men. They accompanied a girl with ragged blonde hair and a dazed, winsome expression. They told me that she was a runaway and that I might have first turn with her, if I would lend the use of my place. The girl offered no resistance. Her vacant eyes veiled a sadness which I suspect only the young can feel, an abandonment which is beyond despair. But my friends were insistent and would have pushed past me if my arm had not been raised to block their entry. They were puzzled and angered by my refusal, and took her away, muttering and shaking their heads in dismay.

Later in the night, I was wakened by what I imagined were her cries—high keening sounds, rising from the fog like tendrils. I rose to peer out my balcony, but Fontana del Re was silent and deserted. "Perhaps it is only the lament of a cat," I thought, and fell backward into a sleep strewn with sorrowful calls.

The social philosophy of the poor Neapolitan is attuned to the imperatives of individual survival. The goals of human endeavor are seen to be self-serving and self-aggrandizing, and the social reality is perceived as agonistic and defensive. The ideal man is capable of monopolizing and wielding physical force. He is adept at subtle psychological manipulations and clever deceptions. He is at once tough, wise, and false, and he is not good at losing. In such a world, the problem of order is never entirely solved, although it is renegotiated continually on the basis of power or its effective pretense. But in contrast to this Hobbesian scheme of social integration, which is a synthesis of negatives, the poor of Naples recognize, with an awareness that is at times tortured, that the requirements of human well-being are rooted in communal support and within networks of positive reciprocity. Their lives are lived out in the tense field of action and feeling that exists between these two polarities. Within this complex of contradictory social processes, social order emerges alternately as an uneasy truce between hostile individuals or as the mutual expression of empathy and need.

chapter four

Tragedies of Fellowship and Community

What good are honor and conscience? You can't put them on your feet instead of boots. Honor and conscience are only good to those who have power—force—

Maxim Gorky, The Lower Depths

Can one know anything about a people by the form of their greeting? Certain Indians of Brazil greet their fellows with the declaration, "I am hungry," thus reinforcing the imperative of commensality.[1] Other peoples may express their reserve with a neutral "Hello" or risk an unwanted intimacy with the query, "How are you?" The poor of Naples say "Addo va?" (Where are you going?). They say it loud and quickly, if they know you, and they expect a quick answer. It is to say that your destinations and their destinations are a matter of mutual concern; that your life and their lives are now somehow intertwined. It is to intrude, immediately and rightfully, into the private sphere of the other. A small and recurrent detail of the moment, it nevertheless dramatizes one of the fundamental contradictions of man's emotional life, thrown into high relief in Naples—that between identity and intimacy, between love which is interdependency, and the will to power of the self.

The Tragic Framework of Community
in the Mediterranean

The Mediterranean is the home of tragedy, and there is nothing accidental in this. Tragedy is the artist's attempt to reconcile the demands of *polis* and *agora* with the psychosocial needs of men. Perhaps this is why the great Athenian tyrant Pisistratus, in the sixth century B.C., chose to elevate the new form to a central position in the public entertainments.[2] Tragedy seeks to make sense of a novel and historically emergent level of social psychology where the problem of man is his singleness in an ever-more complicated and indifferent world, and where the individual is faced with series of desperate choices between competing courses of action.

The primitive world was able to achieve a harmony, unstable at times, between the needs of the individual and the requirements of community. The problems of order, responsibility, and integrity were solved with the problem of bread. But with the advent and dominion in the Mediterranean of a sea-going mercantile capitalism, this harmony is shattered, and tragedy and progress are born to us as twins.

The stratified world of the market, and the warring, tyrannical states which protected it and ravaged it, encouraged the psychic aggression of the individual. Integrity became the special province of the tragic hero. This is the gross psychohistorical framework of Neapolitan and much of Mediterranean history. The rules of survival, for beggar and prince alike, have militated against integrity and have tended to instrumentalize, although not randomize, a majority of human interactions. A picaresque figure like Lazarillo de Tormes, or the antiheroic aristocrat upon whom Machiavelli modeled his Prince, lives by the same code, an antimorality in which integrity as moral responsibility is excluded and dignity is the solace of fools. In Freudian terms, one might say that the aggressive dimension of the personality has been overworked and the ego thrown into confusion. Shame rather than guilt becomes the sanction of social control. In philosophic terms, the individual is left to suffer what F. G. Friedmann has identified as the "peculiar sense of solitude which pervades the whole of southern society."[3] The isolating organization of society forces him to a philosophic turn of mind, leading either to the dullest verbosity or else to a unique and ignescent sense of self, combining grace and power with an awareness of death.

People are not antisocial in the Mediterranean. The honored place of the outsider-guest testifies to the vitality of the social impulse and its frustration within the community of insiders. The locus of tragedy then is not in the death of sociality, but in its nonfulfillment, its futility, and its relegation to yearning. In the ancient and dank back streets of one of the cruelest of the world's cities, people continue to live in communities, albeit broken part-communities, which suffer the egoism of the individual and at the same time relieve him of his immense loneliness.

Polis and Plebs

The people of Fontana del Re did not think of themselves as strangers, colliding with other strangers in an urban nightmare, but rather as citizens of a *polis*, heirs to its distinctively urban legacy of rituals and traditions. The residents of other great Italian cities were their peers in theory, but in truth all things Neapolitan struck them as obviously and indisputably superior. Peasants and rural folk were referred to casually as *i cafoni* (bumpkins). Even middle-class students from the University, if their accents

39

were too provincial, were categorically dismissed as rural hicks, although the superior class standing of any student was usually sufficient to establish his superiority. In a tradition reaching back to the marble cities of Magna Graecia, the rude beggar in the marketplace continues to hold himself higher than the embarrassed peasant newcomer who searches his pockets hurriedly for a coin.

The urban patriotism of lower-class Neapolitans was the only meaningful collective sentiment, regularly expressed, that transcended class boundaries. The daily interactive realities of their lives were determined by placement at the bottom of the social order, and the social relations and groupings which mattered to them were exclusively located inside their own class. The poor of Naples refer to themselves as the *popolino* or "little people." The popolino consititute a communal category in the sense that the blurred boundaries which mark off the urban lower class are the bounds of fellowship and marriage as well. The majority of all marriages at Fontana del Re were between lower-class Neapolitans, born either in the vicinity or in some other lower-class zone. In other words, poor Neapolitans tend to befriend and marry their own kind.

The Neighborhood as a Part-Community

On the feast day of the Madonna del Arco, the Monday after Easter, the people of Fontana del Re joined the *plebs* of Naples in a compelling rite of intensification. Thousands of vehicles, crammed with children and surrounded by noisy congregations of the faithful on foot, jammed the narrow road leading to the shrine, twenty miles outside of Naples. The event was Asiatic in its colors and rhythms. The thousand brightly painted papier-mâché Madonnas, the circles of peasant dancers come out from their farms to entertain the city folk, the ubiquitous firecrackers, the shouting vendors, and finally the treasure-room of the shrine itself, laden with small silver hearts and arms and legs (tokens of gratitude from the cured)—all contributed to impart a vivid sense of the East.

Of sociological interest was the fact that, except for a few aged absentees, the entire population of Fontana del Re and its immediate vicinity was united in one place, behind the banner of the local religious confraternity. Never before had I seen everyone together at once. When we sat down to eat lunch, the men and the boys wondered aloud among themselves whether, as in years past, there would be fighting between the men of different districts. It was then that I began to ask myself to what extent Fontana del Re was a community with some degree of organization, as opposed to a fortuitous and amorphous arrangement of persons. Perhaps the feasting had revealed, within the communal categories of *polis* and class, a mosaic of small part-communities based on daily face-to-face interaction, with territorial limits and loyalties and ritual modes of expressing local solidarity.

Fontana del Re conforms in many ways to the model of the "defended neighborhood" which the sociologist Gerald Suttles has identified as a typical communal form in the social landscape of American cities. According to Suttles, the small neighborhood is staffed by the women, children, and adolescents who pass much of their time there. It is defended by teenage gangs, restrictive convenants, and a "bad" reputation. Suttles refers to "the shared knowledge of an underlife" as a fundamental cognitive feature, and defines the unit as "an emergent and sentimental union of similar people."[4]

The young men of Fontana del Re took an intense interest in their place of residence. They extolled its dubious virtues and sometimes sought protection and sanctuary within its boundaries. It was the young men of the district who investigated me upon my arrival, and it was they who threatened me with expulsion when I failed to serve their interests.

After about eight months at Fontana del Re, I was informed by several young men that if any stranger were to attack me in the vicinity, he would risk the collective vengeance of the local men. I was also told that a middle-class friend of mine, a student with an aloof attitude, was hereafter unwelcome in the quarter and would be shot in the legs from behind if he continued to visit. Rather than test this assertion, I advised the student to meet me elsewhere.

When my friend Pepe deflowered a girl from an adjacent zone and refused to marry her, he risked a severe beating at the hands of her male kin. But he found sanctuary within the walls of Fontana del Re. They would not pursue him beyond its portals.

One day my friend Eduardo took me on a guided tour of the local rubble. As we made our way past various heaps of debris, Eduardo asked rhetorically, over and over again, why no one in city government seemed interested in getting the mess cleared away. At one point, he leaned toward the ground, and tried to re-insert an uprooted paving stone. "I want to die beside my own stones," he said piously as he worked, reminding me of Hollywood's version of the austere peasant, toiling in parched but always beloved fields.

But young Eduardo did not live at Fontana del Re. He had grown up there, but he and his mother, along with a number of other families, had moved away when the building they lived in had threatened to collapse. His mother apparently did not share her son's belief in the beauty of a death in the familiar environs of one's own masonry. She returned every day to Fontana del Re, however, to sell contraband cigarettes. Another woman returned to tend a small candy store. Like Eduardo, the sons of other people who had moved out also "checked in" at Fontana del Re each day to meet with friends. It was many months before I discovered that these people did not actually reside in the neighborhood, so complete was their integration into the local social scene.

The fact that these people belonged as "members" to the neighborhood, without actually residing there, points to a hidden principle of neighborhood organization that may underlie Suttle's notion of a "sentimental union." The mere fact of physical contiguity does not lay a foundation for community. Fontana del Re was more than a neighborhood. It was a place of commerce, where people bought and sold from one another, circulating and recirculating what little capital they had. If one were a vendor, whether in cigarettes, sandwiches, or stolen radios, moving away could involve breaking into another set of closed economic circuits. Certainly it would be easier and safer to retain the niches one already had by professing territorial allegiance to the district where one found one's buyers.

After I had lived for eight months at Fontana del Re, people began to dispense with polite greetings and I was robbed for the first time. These were not signs of rejection but rather tokens of my incorporation into the stream of ordinary interactions and occurrences. I decided that I could at last attempt to take a brief census, a thankless task which yielded only fragmentary results. Eventually I found someone who would assist me. After obtaining repeated assurances of my good intentions, she sat down with me and enumerated the number of people in each apartment, giving their occupations, past and present. The information flowed forth effortlessly. But the next day this woman, a local housewife, informed me that I would never know the secrets of Fontana del Re:

> "Did you think I could tell you the truth, Tommaso, when you asked me all those questions? I had to lie left and right! If you knew how much I had to leave out!"
>
> "You mean, Signora, if you said 'housewife,' you really meant 'whore'?"
>
> "Exactly, things like that."

This is the "shared knowledge of an underlife" referred to by Suttles, which I gradually pieced together from a hundred whispered confidences. How many submerged truths and lies floated up to me thus! Yet their need to reveal this buried knowledge (against the touted virtue of minding one's own business), like their need to scrutinize and probe beneath the surface of a man's face—these were all indices of an ultimate and intense concern for the other. People mattered to one another at Fontana del Re but in a tragically interchangeable sense, as one's opponents or one's friends.

Conflict, Suspicion, and the Meaning of "Friend"

The social exterior of Fontana del Re is apparent on any summer afternoon. Entering the arched lane, you pass by an assemblage of seated old women. Like scrawny black hawks, they sit in place, and take the strong sun. Nearby, four or five young men are hanging about in front of the local bar. The jingle of a pinball machine can be heard faintly from within. Deeper along the winding lane, three children play in a pile of rubble and sand; pieces of old cardboard and scrap metal are their toys. An androgynous boy of nine, with brilliant red hair and white freckled skin, spins about with a bright yellow length of wire in hand to menace the other children. A solitary old woman is dozing on a stool. In a window above, a gaunt young woman, hump-backed and dressed in black, gazes blankly down. From on high, a young mother takes in laundry and chats with another across the clothesline. The white sheets furl about her arms, reflecting the sun's glare with an unexpected tinge of lavender. Suddenly there is a commotion.

The old woman who had been dozing is waving a broom and shrieking after a young man, who turns back to insult her. A second old woman is defending the boy, and a third is bellowing at the second. The housewives above shout their opinions to the crowd gathering below. Some of the young men arrive and join in the shouting. Faces redden. The voices grow louder. Finally, a young woman pushes her way to the side of the first old woman. She is gruff and sturdy, gracious and beautiful at once, and quickly becomes the controlling force of the argument.

By the volume of her voice, the imposing mass of her physique, and the logic of her arguments, the young woman gradually subdues all of the others, including the original young man, to some kind of an agreement. Everyone disperses and, except for an occasional grumble, all is as before, with the old women seated, the children playing, the housewives chatting, and the young men hanging about listlessly in the torpor of the late afternoon.

The argument between the old woman and the boy provides us with an opportunity to see beneath the surface of social life to the structure and quality of underlying relations. Passing by the old woman, the young man had insulted her. She responded by chasing him. The boy's grandmother rose to his defense. The old woman's closest

45

friend rose to hers. The young woman who settled the dispute was the niece of the offended old lady. She demanded respect for her aunt, who was helpless and alone. All agreed that, considering her plight, insults were not called for. The boy was reprimanded.

But why did the boy insult the old woman in the first place and why did she react so vehemently? The old woman had been robbed of her television set a few weeks earlier. She suspected this particular young man. He was aware of her suspicion, and for this reason had insulted her as he passed.

I was told that the old woman had no sons. She was without *"figli guappi"*—strong, tough sons who could retaliate if she were wronged. Therefore she was an ideal victim for the thieves, who were under increasing pressure to confine their criminal activity to the local quarter because of police patrols along the major boulevards. A person without a fierce reputation, or without fierce male kin, was rather helpless at Fontana del Re. The old woman never thought to denounce her suspect to the police. This was an untenable alternative.

This brief episode illuminates the duality of social relations in lower-class Naples. People are close to one another, aware of one another, ready to defend one another, but this same closeness provides opportunities for exploitation as well as protection and aid. Although the old woman was vulnerable to robbery, public opinion could be mobilized in her favor and reprimands issued to those who might otherwise exploit her weakness with total impunity.

One evening I returned to my apartment to find my window shattered and my tape-recorder gone. The tape-recorder proved far more useful to me in absentia than it ever had at my desk. During the following week I was visited by a dozen diverse persons, who secretly confided to me the name of the thief, usually one of the other eleven. I also learned that almost everyone had been robbed at Fontana del Re, and all harbored suspicions about the potential culprits. Stefano told me how his cigarette lighter vanished after his two friends had supper with him. Gennaro told me about Tonino, whose television had disappeared a week earlier. Nothing would be said, but within two months the suspect's portable radio would vanish. The old women whom I passed daily in the street stopped me to commiserate and recount their own experiences of burglarization. Never before had I felt so much a part of the life of Fontana del Re! A few months after the event I saw my tape-recorder, with its distinctive scratches, under the arm of a local *guappo,* or tough guy. I unwisely told a friend, who stupidly told the guappo, who in turn told me that it had been sold to him by some local youths whose names would remain unknown. He expressed sorrow and concern and admonished me to be more selective in my choice of friends. But now I had made an enemy, insofar as he expected some kind of retaliation from me.

What can the word "friend" mean in such a setting? I was often charged with making caffè for my companions. One time, after everyone left, the housepainter Toton returned. He had been sitting on the bed with the others and had lost twenty thousand lire from his back pocket. We searched everywhere but to no avail. Then grimly he pronounced the name of the fellow who had been sitting next to him, certain that his pocket had been picked. He left my apartment muttering to himself and vowing revenge. I felt uneasy. Did he suspect me as well?

The experience of such doubts toward one's fellows, the uneasiness, and the fear of warranted or unwarranted reprisal is the kernel of social experience in lower-class Naples. It is nowhere more apparent than in the social field just beyond kinship, but kin bonds as well are trou-

47

bled by the failure of trust. One night I rose to leave the table of my friend Stefano. It was late. He was tired, and I would be heading for a tavern to meet with some student-friends. But he held me back, insistently, cursing at me in an irritated though not bitter tone. I saw that he was weary and bored. He wanted to talk, to relax with a friend. We resumed our chat, about good times and bad, when Stefano, the junk-man, began to describe the facet of his world-view dealing with friendship:

> "For us, Tommaso, friendships, like taverns, are a luxury. Even though we occasionally eat delicacies, we never confuse them with the food that fills you up. The *popolino*, Tom, not *i grandi signori*—they have their honor—but the *popolino* of here, and of places like Forcella; you know how we are made? To-night, today, I have some money, so I offer you to eat. But tomorrow if I'm broke, and I and my family have to eat, I'll try to rob you and trick you. I'll send you a letter in America and tell you my son is dying, and I need money terribly, and of course, as a *grande signore*, you'll respond. I would try to rob and trick my own brother. But it's easier with friends. Family doesn't help you out anyway, and then, between brothers, if you lend him a hundred thousand lire and he can't pay you back, what can you do? A friend, you can beat his head in. A brother, no. A friend you can revenge yourself against. Don't ever trust anyone Tom, not even me!"

These last words are the sincerest expression of friendship that one man could offer another in the slums of Naples, but there is no elation in comprehending their meaning, only a lingering sadness.

All men yearn for relationships founded on an

48

achieved trust. Even kinship is an empty set of etiquettes if regular interaction does not bring about genuine trust. But trust fails in a world of poverty and socially generated scarcity, and so the relations of community also fail, in terms of what they might otherwise provide. The Spanish philosopher, Miguel de Unamuno, tells us that history develops two kinds of man: the child of hunger and the child of love.[5] And although we can rarely separate the two, in the slums of Naples the child of hunger predominates.

chapter five

Family Life-Worlds

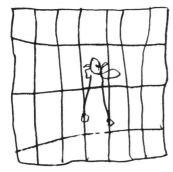

Ciro's drawing of himself, 9/4/74

FAMILY RELATIONS ARE two-faced. They are compounded of care and neglect, affection and abuse, love and hate. They are charged with sensual energy and yet they are defined as asexual. They allocate power to extremes of dominance and subordination, and yet within families (in contrast to more explicitly political formations) power-holders are vulnerable and easily wounded by those who have no power.

Family relations are loose and unspecialized, only to contain unwritten constitutions of rights and obligations. They are structured and formal, and relaxed and informal. They possess a tensile strength unknown elsewhere in society, but all families are destined to break apart. Family feeling seeks to exist above time and beyond death, but as long as they endure, family bonds are menaced by the threats of dissolution and forgetfulness. Men and women

51

think to release their finest potentials as creators and sustainers of families, and yet how often they find their humanity narrowed, enclosed, and trapped by servitude to the dull routines of family life.

Most individuals begin to trace out their first connections to the universe through the intermediary relations of the family. The unique perspective which each person eventually attains on the world is the product of a long succession of interpersonal interactions and private reflections, but the final sum of positives and negatives will always be conditioned by the original assessment, by the emotional values with which the individual begins.

Despite the mythology of sentimental familism that pervades Italian culture, the contradictions of family life in Naples among the poor can be seen with the naked eye. One does not need the special vision of the bourgeois expressionist to perceive the violent clash of motives and the tangled knotting of longings, jealousies, and nourished resentments which form the substrate of so much nuclear family interaction.

In Naples, poverty has compressed the family, tightening it up, overburdening and overheating its linkages. Members of families are drawn to one another by too much need. Material and utilitarian elements threaten always to outweigh the emotional. Balances between autonomy and dependency are disturbed as the necessarily monetized mentality continually refigures the shifting calculus of individual and group well-being. The families of the poor suffer all that families everywhere endure, but the economic ordeal of poverty (as deprivation or insecurity) triggers cycles of implosion leading to explosion which can shatter these families, leaving only part-families and fragments of relationships and persons.

On Sunday afternoons the quarters of Naples are silent and oppressively peaceful. Strolling along the empty lanes, one hears strains of music and the sounds of mingling voices; perhaps the faint clatter of dishes and silverware from the open windows and balconies above. By thus perceiving the sounds and signs of life from afar, by the stillness and solitude of the streets, by the closed façades of shops and stalls, and by the overriding image of a world withdrawn from public view, far into its private essence, one is forced to conclude that the elementary unit of social life in Naples is the family.

Does this mean that the Neapolitan family is a haven of solidarity and cooperation in a world which threatens always to exploit and maim the individual? My personal experience of family in Naples suggests that this is not so. The family is a haven in the same sense that, in bad weather, a prison is a haven. The facts of scarcity and the consequent failures of solidarity and trust, and the recurrent themes of suspicion, cruelty, and violence which stain the lives of the poor, do not stop at the barricades of the family but rather collect and fester at this critical node. The realities of family life in Naples are very different from their commonly accepted idealization.

First Exposures

In an urban setting as densely populated as central Naples, the fieldworker is confronted with a blinding variety of personalities and groups. This variety frustrates the search for common structures and shared patterns. Moreover, most anthropological fieldworkers do not choose their informants. Their informants choose them, and in a place like central Naples one counts oneself lucky to have been chosen at all. I cannot know if the families whose private worlds I was allowed to penetrate are representative of the norm or not. I can compare my own observations with those of others but I cannot attain a high order of generality.

As my research in Naples stumbled through its erratic early phase, I despaired of ever touching, in any meaningful way, the inner surfaces of life in the poor quarters. Before I was given the opportunity to know one family intimately, I had collected only a sparse and discontinuous series of glances and fragmentary impressions. It was as if I had found, here and there in the street, torn and damaged snapshots of various families and from these was supposed to piece together some kind of cultural understanding. But these snapshots were not posed, and for this reason they are valuable insofar as they forced me to reject the sentimental tableaux which I suspect I had been searching for in those early days. Two of these "snapshots," however, were clear and vivid and sufficiently intact to reproduce here.

Before settling in at Fontana del Re, early one evening in mid-May I set off for a customary meandering stroll with my friend and guide, Carlo. Passing by the U.S.O. headquarters, a tawdry place on a littered alley, we saw two small boys lingering about, stopping the sailors and begging for change. The smaller boy clung tenaciously to the older. I would estimate their ages at 7 and 11. They wore no shirts. They were thin but not emaciated. The pants of the older boy were over-sized and torn, held up by an old belt. His shoes were a shredding of laces and soles. The clothing of the other was no better. They were both filthy, tanned with dirt, and they smelled, a sharp, pungent human smell.

Carlo asked them if they were hungry. We brought them to a nearby pizzeria. The owner questioned our entry, but allowed us to remain. We fed them pizzas and some orange soda. The older boy, Guido, asked me a series of questions about America. He spoke Italian as well as the dialect. He had learned Italian, he told me, at the *Istituto*. His eyes were dark and alert. He asked about the sensation of riding in an airplane. He asked me about *giustizia* (justice) in America, "Do they have any there? Could you take me back with you?"

It was getting dark, and the spring evening was turning cold. As we left the restaurant, the two boys began to shiver. They locked arms and clung to one another more tenaciously than ever. After much argument and after guaranteeing that they would not be beaten, Carlo convinced them to let us escort them back home to their mother. They had run away two days before.

We started to walk them home, attracting attention along the way. Even in poor Naples they were a sight, recalling the gangs of *scugnizzi* (street urchins) who roamed the streets in the postwar period. We climbed up the steep slope of the old quarter to a kind of cliff-dwelling complex of structures, overlooking all of Naples. The shabby rooftops were iridescent in the dimming twilight. The distant glass dome of the Galleria glowed like a lantern.

As we scrambled up the steps, some boys gathered. To my confusion they began to scoff, jeering and pointing obscenely. Carlo stopped for a moment to speak with them while I waited up ahead with the boys.

We finally arrived at a small *basso* set on a dirt courtyard. A short woman with a mannish face appeared at the entrance. Her hair was black and clipped short. She wore a pink skirt with a broken zipper, and a pink sweater. Her lips were thin; her eyes were black and small.

When we entered, she said nothing but looked at her sons with a stare of accusation and reproach. She expressed neither joy nor relief at the sight of them. She addressed herself to Carlo and me, repeatedly drawing a sharp line between her innocence and their guilt. Silently she led Carlo over to a closet to show him pairs of new trousers and shirts, none of which appeared to have ever been worn. She opened the refrigerator and took out a beefsteak for our inspection. She asked us to sit down and offered us some beer and began to talk in a dreary chant-like monotone.

I looked around the one room. The air was tainted with the odors of kitchen grease and unwashed bedding. The matrimonial bed filled almost the entire room but left space for a small table and a dresser. Above the bed was an electrified image of the Sacred Heart. Various cheap knickknacks and a large blue perfume bottle decorated the room. The "bathroom," a toilet behind a curtain, was set beside the stove near the door. In one corner a snappy dog guarded a new litter of pups. A child was asleep on the bed, a little girl of three or four. The mother told us that the child had recently been blinded in one eye in an accident while playing. Now she had a fever. The two boys, she said, were not permitted to sleep on the bed. They were too filthy. They could sleep on the floor with the dogs.

The woman continued to speak, sighing intermittently. Although she was complaining, I heard no emotion in her voice, no anger, no passion. Her skin was pale, almost gray, and except for the sighs she remained expressionless.

She complained about the law and the police. Guido had stolen a bird from a cage in a pet shop. He had been caught and the police had brought him to her for reprimanding. The incident, they told her, was too trivial for prosecution. "Why didn't they bring him to jail instead? He belongs in jail!" She meant it. She went on to discuss the problem of finding work for the boys and the problem of keeping them in school. Guido had spent six years in the *Istituto* and that was good. She complained about their father, whom she expected home soon. She related the story of her recent miscarriage. It had happened while she was searching the streets for her runaway sons. It would be their sin.

Carlo offered to help find the older boy a job. We rose to leave. When we said good-bye, the two boys were playing in the corner with the dog and the pups.

On the way back, Carlo told me why the other boys had scoffed. Young Guido, they said, often went with older men, to earn a few lire. They had been eager to give details. I wondered what would happen to this strange bright child, who risked imprisonment to steal a bird. I thought about his mother and her apparent exhaustion and her flesh-tones like stone. As we descended the hill, the old quarter was vague and phosphorescent beneath a rising moon, while across the bay was the silhouette of Vesuvius, massive and stark against the night sky, as though brooding.

Angela had married Michele six years ago, when she was seventeen. She was a small woman, with high delicate cheekbones and fine, light brown hair. She had striking almond eyes and a ready smile. Michele was twelve years older than she. He was balding slightly and getting paunchy. He read books occasionally and was a fervent Communist. Laughing, he was slightly uneasy, as though caught in some momentary contradiction with himself.

Michele and Angela lived in an inexpensive apartment in a lower-class district of Naples with their two baby sons. Michele was a dressmaker and worked out of his apartment-workshop from seven to seven, six days a week.

Angela assisted Michele all day long, preparing patterns, cutting cloth, pinning and sewing, and occasionally running out to deliver an order. She also made the morning and afternoon caffè, cleaned the apartment, did all the daily marketing, cooked all meals, washed diapers and clothes, and cared for the boys. She had no female kin to help her. Her mother had died when she was young, and she had no sisters.

Michele's long hours indoors were wearying to him. On most nights, after finishing supper he would go out to chat with friends or see a movie. Angela stayed home, however, to clean up and put the babies to sleep and perhaps watch some television before going to bed.

I often met and talked with Michele and his friends. I recall once coming to their apartment and seeing Angela at the end of a typical day. She was haggard and pale. I saw the future lines of her face, harsh like a net on her soft features. Her infant son was cradled at her breast, half-asleep.

"I love them when they're so small like this," she told me. "They understand only the mother at this age. No one else."

Michele loved his children intensely, but I do not know if he loved his wife. In his mind she was somehow linked with all that held him down and oppressed him. He often complained about her inability to understand him. Occasionally, perhaps melodramatically, he confided that he remained alive only for his children.

During the day the three-year-old, Giacomino, would get into everything. He wielded scissors and knives as readily and as menacingly as less lethal toys. These objects would sometimes be taken away by his parents, but the boy's aggression, like his flirtations with danger, was only rarely discouraged. Yet neither was his capacity to love and show affection discouraged. When encouraged to kiss me, he did. He was endlessly playful and showed little fear or uneasiness in the presence of a stranger. He felt intense jealousy for his newborn brother, however, and had scratched the sleeping infant's face more than once. For this his father spanked him, although not harshly. Angela was patient but stern. She understood that the boy felt threatened by his sudden displacement from the center of the stage. Even with her multitudinous chores, she made a special effort to give him extra attention and reassure him of her love.

I remember once when Angela dyed her hair red. She had wanted to make it blond but that would have involved touch-ups, which are time-consuming and costly. After dyeing her hair she eagerly anticipated Michele's response, but upon seeing her he became irritated and told her that she looked like a whore.

Angela could not think of leaving Michele. She had no place else to go and knew of no other respectable way to survive.

One Neapolitan Family in Close-up

In an economic sense, the family is for sharing and pooling and distributing. The family is an organizational innovation to facilitate feeding, and by the (implicit) directives of the incest taboo to insure the species a steady supply of genetically vigorous and politically useful mates. But the family is more than a set of arrangements for food-sharing and alliance formation, more than a corporation for the husbandry of reproductive potentials. The family is the crucible of every human identity.

Like each person, every family has a distinctive quality. Each family imposes its own collective being upon the isolate being of each of its members. Each family sets up a different pendulum swing between the polarizing emotions of man. The family remains a mystery because it can be reduced neither to its particular cultural form nor to its

59

historically determined functions. It can no more be accounted for by its individual components than these can be accounted for by it. Here the whole is more than the sum of the parts and every part is more than the whole. There is a trace element in human consciousness whose presence can be detected as much in a set of relationships as in a work of art. It is the element which is aware and decisive and creative or destructive as it decides and chooses to create or destroy.

I came to know one family in Naples well, not as a cultural form and not as a set of historically determined functions, although these I hope will be apparent in the details of their interactions. I came to know and feel the life-pulse of one poor Neapolitan family, and the violent rocking backward and forward of it, as it moved through its own life-world, and as it was enveloped in ever more dense and concentric atmospheres of time.

Scenes from a Family's Life

The setting. A large dining room with cracked plaster walls. There is a window-balcony, but half of the panes are broken. An intricate, leafy, but fading wallpaper covers one wall. For furniture, there is a mahogany china-closet and a side-table and mirror, arched with family photographs. A chandelier with pendants of bright red glass hangs over a large wooden table; a number of wobbly chairs are ranged around. In one corner, a television set is blaring. High in another corner, two yellow canaries hop about in a simple wooden cage.

The participants. Stefano, the father: He is a junk-collector by trade; an unshaven man about forty years old, with black thinning hair and small ink-black eyes.

Elena, the mother: Her face, like her form, is wide and thick-set, with definite straight-drawn lines. She wears a stained apron over a plain black dress, and no make-up.

Gennaro, the oldest son: A young man of eighteen with a lean, powerful frame and course rough-hewn features.

Ciro, the second son: He is a tall, thin adolescent of fifteen, with long arms and legs which seem to confound him as often as they serve. His smile is broad and clownish, marred by a missing front tooth. He suffers from a mild rash on his chin.

Pasquale, the third son: A thirteen-year-old boy with limpid, tender eyes and pure pale coloring. His smiles are eager and seem almost to tremble on his lips, as though in anticipation of some secret gift. His head is tilted at an unusual angle to his body.

Nina, the daughter: She is a pretty eleven-year-old with large eyes and a wide mouth. She has a quick, elfin manner.

Giuseppe, age ten, is a soft cub of a boy with brown eyes and sandy hair.

Robertino is a ruddy-faced, hyperactive five-year-old with an expression that is alternately sweet and demonic.

1. A Boy Who Will Not Work

It is a Sunday afternoon in October. Everyone is assembled at the table, devouring huge bowls of pasta and potatoes. Ciro hesitates and stutters, then requests a cigarette from his father. Stefano says nothing. His jaws shift about as he finishes his food.

"You are a *cretino*." The word is like a razor. "Do you understand? A creti-i-no!" The other children titter. Gennaro sneers. Ciro looks away, when suddenly Stefano's voice blows out in a shattering explosion. "Man of shit—you eat and sleep and that's all you can do—good-for-nothing little bastard!" He turns to address me, nearly out of breath, still shouting.

"Do you know, Tommaso, why I love my son Gennaro

61

so much? Because he's been working for ten years, that's why. But this cretino here, he hasn't worked a day."

Gennaro flexes with pride. He regards his younger brother with contempt. Ciro pushes his chair out.

"What the fuck are you looking at?" he asks indignantly. The little ones fall back delighted. "A fight, a fight"; they clap and giggle. In an instant, Gennaro pounces and seizes Ciro by the neck, pinning his head against the table. The boy's long arms swing and flail, but he is helpless. Gennaro taunts him with his subjection.

Stefano swoops up from his seat. Pushing Gennaro aside, he rains blows down upon Ciro, whipping him with slaps, and driving him into a corner beneath the frantic birds. Hoarse sobs croak up from the boy's lungs; desperate cries that claw at the air and bring a hush to the room. Stefano thunders at the son cowering before him. His voice cracks midway into a whisper, a gasp: "Don't cry! Don't cry, or I will kill you." So the odd choking noises cease, and the boy only trembles without making a sound.

Elena has sat watching in silence. Her arms are folded. Her expression is grim. She bellows at the defeated child, commanding him to bed, and turns to confront Gennaro. He looks away from her.

"Are you proud, big man? Such a big, strong man! Get out!" Gennaro exits. Elena tramps into the kitchen, to return in a few moments with plates of sweet fried sausage and chilled, home-pickled tomatoes. Stefano admonishes me to eat. We break bread, and he refills my glass with wine. After serving the other children, Elena joins us at the table. Stefano pauses to speak about Ciro.

"I'm a good father, Tommaso, but my kids don't know it. When Ciro ran away to Rome—*disgraziato* that he is—and the priest called me to fetch him, I dropped everything to go get him. As soon as I arrived in Rome, I telephoned him, and you know Tommaso, he wouldn't speak to me: me, his own father, and he wouldn't come to the phone! How I cried, Tommaso! In front of the Romans, in the street. I swear it."

Elena interrupts: "He has to work because we can't make ends meet if he doesn't. The little ones can't contribute yet. Gennaro works in a gas station around the corner. He gives me twenty thousand lire of every thirty he earns. But this other *stronzo*—he runs away! Do you think he's neglected here? Do you think he lacks for anything?" (Elena leads me into the adjacent bedroom and points to a bunk bed.) "Gennaro sleeps in the top bunk and Ciro shares the bottom with Pasquale here." She pulls away some blankets, proud to reveal the clean sheets below. "So you see Tommaso, he's well taken care of here."

Pasquale makes a face and holds his nose. "You should sleep with those feet in your face. The gorgonzola, phew, the gorgonzola!"

"Pasquale, why not shut your face and make us some caffè." Pasquale plods into the kitchen, returning shortly with a dented pot of steaming thick espresso. He pours it carefully into the little glasses and serves with all the hauteur and efficiency of a rich man's butler. From a paper bag, Elena pours a pile of greenish walnuts onto the table. Little Giuseppe comes to my side. His sandy hair is as soft and delicate as cornsilk. His mother screams at him to stop pestering me. Nina is resting in her father's arms and Rob is nestled happily against Elena's wide breast. Occasionally, he aims a nut at his sister. For every miss, she gives a shriek; for every hit, a loud, irritating wail. Soon, everyone is quiet for a popular television show. Stefano begins to doze in his chair, while Pasquale and his mother clear the table and clean up. I bid all good night and depart.

2. Secret Agent

Ciro and I are playing a simple game of cards. Whenever I win, he declares my victory null and void. When he wins, he grins and laughs triumphantly, anxious to continue.

Pasquale enters with knives, forks, and plates. His face is sour and anemic, swollen at the right cheek. He greets me sullenly, and is slow to set the table.

"Speed it up, dimwit," his mother snaps. Pasquale puts his hands to his cheek.

"O-o-oh, poor boy," she mocks him. "He thinks he can fool me, Tommaso. Just look at him. Oh, but I understand this one too well; every gesture!" Her face sets hard against him. "Watch, Tommaso, I'll kill him one day!" She turns again to Pasquale and sighs, "Oh God, how you are ugly! Who made you?" But Pasquale ignores his mother's disdain and protests to me that he has a toothache.

The children assemble around the table. Ciro is whistling and humming to himself. From the corner of my eye, I note that Robertino is tiptoeing toward him from behind. Suddenly the air is rent by a quick, sharp crack. Ciro slips from his chair and sinks to the floor. Rob has surprise-attacked him with a broomstick.

Stefano enters the room in time to witness Rob's attack. He nods at Ciro; "A shot in the head? It'll do you good." Stefano smiles to reassure me. "Don't be alarmed, Tommaso. We all have to suffer the antics of the little ones." It was then I recognized the child as an agent of parental terror.

Elena serves the first course, of *macaroni al ragu*. As usual, she serves me first, then Stefano, then Gennaro, and then, in a break with custom, she skips over Ciro to serve the other children before him.

"And why me last?" he protests.

"Because you're a shit. That's why," she responds, effectively cutting off all further discussion.

The room is lively with sounds of eating and the erratic chirping of Stefano's canaries. Gennaro is seated beside me. He is thoroughly absorbed with his macaroni, and attacks it frenetically, like an enthused, clumsy lover. Stefano empties a bottle of beer into a half-filled pitcher of wine, a procedure, he tells me, which improves as it carbonates the wine.

Robertino receives some beer-wine, as does everyone else. Elena collects the dishes, to return momentarily with plates of fried cutlets, accompanied by servings of sweet, fried peppers—green, red, and gold, beneath a glistening amber haze. When I compliment the Signora on her culinary skills, Stefano is pleased and proceeds to tell me about all the wonderful dishes that they will prepare in the coming year.

"It is the season of the pork, Tommaso. Wait till you taste my wife's *zuppa forte* and the sausages we make."

Ciro joins in. "Papa, tell him about Christmas."

So Stefano tells me of the Christmas feasting and all that I shall miss if I fail to join them. Everyone listens with anticipatory joy, as their father conjures up visions of food which are wondrous and magical.

Gennaro tears away at his cutlet with hands and teeth. The others work with implements. After finishing his cutlet, Gennaro makes an announcement: he intends to take boxing lessons and has enrolled in a course at a local gym. Stefano's outburst is deafening, as he condemns his son for assuming that he can spend money on such luxuries. But Gennaro stands up to defy his father, and for an instant, the two men are locked together in a stare of hate. Elena hurls her steak-knife like a spear, across the table, but Gennaro dodges it. "Go fuck yourself," she hollers, "but don't bust our balls." The young man is subdued. Peace returns when Elena emerges from the kitchen to set down a platter of hot potato croquettes, toast-colored and filled with melted mozzarella cheese.

Everyone grabs at these with gusto, especially Robertino, whose mouth and cheeks quickly overflow with this,

his favorite food. Stefano begins to tell jokes, firing them off in rapid succession. Elena and the children are doubled over with laughter, but I cannot understand the rapid flow of dialect. Stefano and his sons narrate each joke again, very slowly, for my benefit. If I fail to respond with the appropriate guffaws, they patiently repeat the joke again. They want very much for me to laugh with them.

Elena puts out nuts and grapes. Pasquale is told to make the caffè. When he slumps and drags more than usual, his mother concedes that he might indeed be ill. Stefano consoles him: "Afterward, go to bed. But now we need the caffè. Understand?" While Pasquale prepares the caffè, I ask whether or not he will require a dentist.

"What dentist, Tommaso? Bed!" Apparently Elena believes in the curative properties of sleep, as the least expensive and most effective of remedies. She goes on to expand upon her medical skills.

"You might put a band-aid on a kid's toe, Tommaso, and for this, they all get on line around here. But I can take care of anything. Gennaro woke up with a fever this morning. You wouldn't know it now. *Va bene.* He couldn't go when he woke up, so I gave him a pill and he went. Then I gave him another pill, and he went some more. Now he feels great. Don't you, Gennaro?" Had he been on his deathbed, Gennaro would have been hard put to contradict her, but he looked healthy enough and nodded appreciatively.

Stefano was getting drowsy. Before I departed, I saw that Ciro seemed to have recovered from Rob's broomstick attack. He seized the boy and forced him to accept a sloppy wet kiss. Rob resisted with slaps and kicks and spit directly into Ciro's face. Ciro laughed and teased the child with a flurry of light slaps. At one point, when Robertino adopted a karate-like stance and clenched his fists in the oriental manner, Stefano started up from his chair to shout, "Kung fu, Rob, Go! Go!" delighted by this evidence of the child's tough and resourceful spirit.

3. Bright Eyes

An additional guest is present. Raffaello is a young man, old before his time, with yellow teeth and thick greasy hair. He is an occasional helper to Stefano. I am told that he lives and sleeps in his cart, underneath the cardboard he collects for a living.

As she serves the first course of macaroni, Elena informs Raffaello that his old friend, little Giuseppe, has made him a cuckold.

"You're not his favorite anymore. He has a new friend now." She smiles at the boy and at me, as though to bestow her blessing. But Raffaello will yield to no competitor. He approaches Giuseppe to tickle him. The boy wriggles away, suppressing a giggle. Elena, Ciro, and Pasquale encircle him.

"Tell us who you like the best?" They are determined to have an answer. When Giuseppe remains silent, his mother commands him to choose. The boy inches closer to Raffaello. Everyone teases me for having lost out.

The Signora sets down my plate, brimming with macaroni, simultaneously with Raffaello's. Stefano praises his friend as a fine helper and companion, referring to him, perhaps too often, as "a good boy." Laughing uneasily, Stefano refers to a debt of 8,000 lire which he hopes Raffaello will soon be in position to pay back.

During the second course of chilled pot roast, Robertino slips from his seat and disappears beneath the table. Everyone continues eating, as though nothing were amiss, but the atmosphere is electric. In an instant, Nina is howling. Everyone ignores her. Rob surfaces, to resume his post beside his mother. When Elena leaves the room to prepare more food, Nina turns upon Giuseppe. The two of them fall to the floor, grunting, squealing, and laughing, and finally whining in unison. Rob hovers about to deliver playful kicks. Elena emerges from the kitchen with a platter of fried eel. She sidesteps the squirming knot of bodies and nods to Stefano.

Like a stand of deer who have been alerted to an unseen danger, the children cease their fighting and scatter. Stefano reaches for his bamboo fishing pole, and circles the room, bending and snapping the pole like a bull whip. The children tremble and crouch. Order is restored for the pastries and the caffè.

As usual, Pasquale collects the dishes, and prepares and serves the caffè. He is muttering to himself and is apparently troubled. His eyes, normally clear, are gray and murky. When he accidently knocks over a glass, Elena reaches across the table and slaps him across the face with the back of her hand.

"A slap is for calming, Tommaso," she explains. She turns to Ciro. "How you are disgusting!" she says. His mouth is smeared with cannoli cream. He retaliates by feigning an aristocratic daintiness, before losing himself completely in a fit of slobbering.

After caffè, Raffaello amuses himself by teasing Robertino. The boy responds by sending a wad of spit into Raffaello's face. Elena orders Raffaello to stop. When he persists, she screams at him, "Lay off!" Raffaello pays no attention and Rob wails pathetically, eyeing his mother and adjusting his decibel level as he gauges her readiness to defend him. Raffaello gives the sign of the cuckold. The boy's cry rises and in an instant Elena is between the man and the boy, shoving Raffaello and striking him with her fists. Stefano rushes to Raffaello's aid. He pulls Rob loose from Elena's skirts and suspends the boy in the air by his feet. Raffaello makes faces and Stefano plants a kiss, turning to a bite, on the child's exposed bottom. The boy kicks and gnashes wildly at anything in his reach. Elena is frantic to rescue him. She sinks her teeth into Stefano's forearm. Stefano gives a deathly moan and releases the captive child.

"See how you like it!" she hollers, as she grabs Rob and hustles him off to the bedroom.

Stefano and Raffaello calm down with some brandy, and chuckle furtively, for fear of Elena's wrath. Stefano invites Raffaello and me to the movies. He plans to treat Elena and the children. In about fifteen minutes, Elena reappears, nudging Rob forward. His cheeks are shining and his hair is slicked. He is dressed in his best clothes. As we flatter him, he turns about in the midst of us with his arms held out. His face is irradiated by our praise. I see his bright eyes dancing.

4. "All of My Children Are 'Bravo!'"
Elena sets down the bowls, heavy again with pasta. The lines of her face are like gashes. She complains of a headache which has tormented her for three days. Stefano motions to the wine bottle and admonishes me to refill my glass. I am pleased but also embarrassed by the implicit familiarity and carefully pour the wine.

Robertino has a new toy, an enormous plastic hammer with a compressible accordion head. It seems to have been custom-made for Rob, who could now pummel as many heads as he wished without fear of blood reprisals. Ciro's skull is Rob's target of choice, and the hammer soon finds its mark. Ciro is startled and dazed. His arms fly into the air like two drugged birds, and my glass, full of wine, finds its way into Stefano's lap. Stefano glowers at Ciro, but Ciro as quickly points to me as the culprit, thus capping a volcanic measure of paternal wrath.

"Don't worry about it, Tommaso. Pour yourself another glass." Dutifully I pour, but within a few moments, as though in obedience to some migratory instinct, Ciro's arms are waving and fluttering over my glass to do their awful work once more. Ciro vanishes, and Stefano, looking up from the purple tablecloth, warns me with his eyes that his patience is wearing thin.

"Take another glass, Tommaso. Drink."

By now, Elena has transformed the landscape of her table. Everywhere, there are rolling hills of pasta, fed by rivers and streams of butter and cheese and sauce. This new environment has a calming effect on everyone. Stefano looks up at me with an expression of affectionate reproach and accuses me of disloyalty. I shall forget them all when I return to America. When I protest loudly, as though offended, Stefano is satisfied and appears relieved. But Elena interrupts. Her voice is uncommonly gentle and sad.

"No, Tommaso, you will forget us. If you settled here it might be different, but you will forget us when you go away. I know, because this is what my brother in London has done. He makes plenty, but we never see a dime of it. When my mother was alive, he wrote all the time. He sent packages, and once in a while he came to visit. But since my mother died, we never hear a word. It's as if he died too." Now Elena is on the verge of tears.

"If my mother were alive, Tommaso, she would have fussed and gone on about you, because you look like him. But though I loved my mother well, she never did right by me. When she was on her deathbed, she wanted a different dish every day, and whatever she wanted, I worked hard to make her happy. But she preferred my younger sister, and always left me to go it alone. She hated Stefano. But that was tough shit on her. When he nearly died of nosebleed, of all things, she wouldn't cough up a dollar for the medicine. If it weren't for St. Anthony, he'd be six feet under. And when I had Rob, and it was a difficult birth, she got up and left the room, just when we needed the surgeon. She said, 'Who is going to pay for this child?' Luckily, I'd put a little money aside. Ahh, but she was good in her own way. How I loved her!''

Changing the subject, I ask the Signora if her sister and two brothers, who resided nearby, could be relied upon in emergencies.

"The brother in the basso around the corner, with the daughter . . . He is *infamo*, Tommaso. Don't ever cross him. His temper is ugly. With all his connections to the contraband, he's doing fine. But do you think he ever sends a banana our way? And the other one with the juice stand on the corner. He's got piles of money, but he's a stingy bastard too. My sister sells cigarettes here at Fontana del Re. You know her. The humpback. Wanna marry her?'' For a moment, Elena is all mirth and laughter. Stefano and the others giggle and titter.

"Anyway, my sons buy from her all the time. She won't even sell one pack to Gennaro on credit! We mind our own business, Tommaso. It's better that way. If I'm in trouble, I'll go beg from the nuns before I ask them for a nickel. Of course, when they have trouble, oh boy, do we ever hear about it!''

Robertino squeals. Ciro is having his revenge. He has pulled down the boy's pants, and is grabbing him at the crotch.

"Look everyone, look at what a beautiful prick my brother has!'' Rob retaliates by twisting Ciro's nose, with a single decisive wrench. He leaps to freedom and dashes to his mother's lap. But Elena is tired. Ciro is holding his nose and snarling. Elena looks imploringly at Stefano. "I can't make it anymore,'' she moans. "I just can't make it.'' Still, she strokes Rob's hair. His lower lip is pushed out to dramatize his sense of outrage. Elena whispers in his ear, to soothe him, "mussel soup, Easter cake. . . .''

71

Soon she rises to get the second course, a cold bean salad with sliced hard-boiled eggs. She apologizes to me; "I'm too tired to cook today." But no sooner has everyone finished than she is on her feet again. This time she returns with a platter of fried rice-balls filled with melted cheese.

Gennaro bursts into the room, accompanied by his friend, Pepe. Naples has won the soccer game. Everyone listens intently to his detailed report. Elena sets plates of macaroni in front of Gennaro and Pepe. They eat ravenously. Gennaro's boisterous energy and simple sense of well-being pervade the room. Stefano beams at him.

"This is my favorite, Tommaso. He's got a good head. The others? Well, who knows why but their heads aren't so good. But maybe Gennaro will make good, own his own bar someday, or go to America. That would be fine, and you could be his sponsor. If he went, we could all go, and you could help us find a place. We could all live together!"

I offer all possible assistance. Since Ciro seems dejected, I direct attention to him.

"And Ciro could come with Gennaro. He is *bravo*." Ciro is about to grin when his mother's voice rings out:

"And the others? The others aren't?"

(I am confused.)

"They aren't bravo also? Only Ciro?"

I try to explain.

"All are bravo, Tommaso."

"Yes, of course, I only meant. . . ."

"All of my children are bravo." She regards her assembled brood with a self-satisfied smile. She is pompous and self-congratulatory.

Stefano breaks the tension. He protests to all present what a good father he has been to his children. He tells me the story of Ciro and Rome again and recounts how he wept in the street.

"How I cried, Tommaso!" Elena commiserates with Stefano's sense of injustice. "Do you see, Tommaso, what we suffer for our children?"

Stefano turns to Pepe. "Look, Pepe, you know how much I like your papa, and don't misunderstand, I would be the last person to say anything bad about him, but haven't I been a better father than him?" Pepe, whose mouth is stuffed with rice balls, nods enthusiastically. He has a notoriously bad relationship with his father.

Elena commands Pasquale to his usual tasks. He mumbles erratically as he collects the plates. But when he takes my dish, he pauses, to announce that he has been studying diligently of late, all manner of subjects. In rapid succession, he recites the birthdates of Columbus, Garibaldi, and Victor Emmanuele II, and proceeds to explain some of the details of pulmonary circulation. "Am I right or not, Tommaso?"

But if I seem impressed with these intellectual pyrotechnics, Stefano is not. "Well, just listen to the doctor! Doctor my ass! Now make the coffee, shithead." Pasquale is jolted back to reality by his father's words and sulks back into the kitchen. When he returns with the coffee, wearing an apron, Nina starts to giggle. Ciro understands, and together the two of them tease, "Fairy, fairy." Gennaro and Pepe are quick to join in, and hoot in high-pitched tones. Stefano laughs in spite of himself. Nina is unrelenting with her mocking litany. Even Rob gets into the act, stalking Pasquale's apron and raising it as though it were a skirt. The hilarity is universal. Pasquale turns crimson, then ashen. His eyes fill up with tears. He looks to Elena for deliverance, but she turns away, covering her mouth in a futile attempt to conceal her laughter. When

73

Ciro parades and swishes past him, Pasquale loses control, and lashes out with fists and curses. He smashes Ciro in the face and slaps Nina. Gennaro leaps up from his chair in defence of his sister. Stefano is on his feet, undoing his belt.

Pasquale begs his father in vain for mercy. Stefano is unmoved and orders him into the other room. He removes his belt and follows the child into the bedroom. The others are silent. Rob giggles uneasily. A stillness, a foreboding, descends over the room like a poison vapor, as we each keep count of Pasquale's fearful screams.

5. *Pieces of the Heart*

It is a cool night in late October. Because it is a weeknight, the scene shifts to the kitchen. Elena is busy at the stove. Stefano and I are sipping some *anice*, a liqueur. Stefano is exhausted after a heavy day of moving work. His entire frame sags toward the floor. Robertino cuddles on his lap. Stefano kisses the child and strokes him as he tells me about his day. He is very glad to be home.

Stefano recalls with me good years and bad. For him, this has been a good year. He shows me the food which they are putting up for the winter. He points to a homemade salami, coiled and hanging from a nail on the wall like some household serpent-god. He reveals trays of green tomatoes and peppers *sott' olio,* under oil. He insists that I sample the stringbeans and the eggplant, marinating *in bottiglia.* He opens the lower cupboards to reveal large sacks of beans and rice and green coffee beans.

Stefano tells Elena that he would like the pickled tomatoes as a side dish for supper. But Elena turns around to ask the smaller children which they would prefer, the tomatoes or the stringbeans. As though rehearsing for a commercial, Giuseppe, Nina, and Rob shout for the stringbeans. Elena shrugs, "What can I do? The kids want string-beans." Laughing quietly, she reaches for the bottle. Stefano accepts defeat.

"And who do you like more Rob, Mama or Papa?" He croons at the boy, but Rob is unflinching in his allegiance to Mama and hugs at her skirts.

"Doesn't anyone love me more?" Stefano pleads, winking at me. Only Nina seems moved and rushes into her father's arms. But just as quickly, uncertain of the practical wisdom of her decision, she abandons Stefano and joins the other side.

Ciro is just home from work. He has found a job as a bartender's assistant. Having witnessed Nina's defection, he addresses me with mock professorial solemnity.

"Of fathers, how many there are, Tommaso, but of mothers, there is only one. . . . But how I love this father of mine!" He throws his arms around Stefano's neck, and gives him a sloppy kiss on the cheek. But Stefano is fumbling with Ciro's long rubbery arms, trying desperately to throw them off. "It would be enough if you just got lost!" he shouts.

Elena sets out the bowls of macaroni with cauliflower. Within the hour Gennaro arrives, followed soon by Pasquale. She sets out bowls for them as well, while Stefano, myself, and the little ones receive servings of fried sausage and pickled stringbeans. Elena takes the remaining macaroni from the pot and places it in the center of an enormous crust of bread. This is her supper.

Robertino has donned his Zorro costume. He leaps about the table with black cape and flexible plastic sword. He sets upon the others without warning, lashing them across the back and scalp. When Nina screams to Stefano, her voice quavering with fear, Stefano reprimands Rob. But then he bids the whining boy to his side and lifts him to his lap. He tousles the child's hair and dares him, half in jest, to take a bite from his arm. Rob waits, but a few moments later he sinks his teeth into his father's flesh. Stefano's curses set the table trembling, but the offender is never punished. Shaking his head, Stefano turns to me: "Ahh, Robertino is terrible, Tommaso. He's awful. That's clear. But he's ours. If someone else gives him a slap, it's a slap to me. If they don't want him, they don't want me. We stay home a lot because of this."

Raffaello arrives to ask Stefano about his work plans for the week. Elena orders Pasquale to prepare the caffè.

Pasquale groans. His arm is too sore for work, he claims, because of a blow delivered by Elena the day before. He pulls up his sleeve to exhibit a large black and blue mark. For a moment, Elena is dumbfounded. She sits in her place, stony and impassive. But in the space of a second, her gray eyes catch fire like dry kindling, and she is after the boy! He turns and flees. She pursues, like a mad elephant on the rampage. Round and round the table they run, while the others make way. She falls upon him, and his face wrenches as she screws a fork into his shoulder. Finally she takes a loaf of bread from the table and, wielding it like a truncheon, she finishes him off. Pasquale drags himself away, whimpering and moaning, into the other room. No caffè is prepared.

Robertino attacks Ciro with his black whip-sword. Ciro laughs defiantly. Together, he and Rob join forces against Giuseppe who, for the moment, seems to enjoy being set upon. Rob leaps like an acrobat into the air, and comes down on Giuseppe's face. When Giuseppe twists Rob's ear, Ciro strikes Giuseppe. Nina kicks Ciro, and Rob jabs at Nina. Ciro comes to Rob's side and threatens Nina, but Gennaro takes her part and slaps Ciro. The room is filled with grunts and cries. Rob, Giuseppe, and Nina whine for their mother, but Elena is beyond caring.

She is dejected and inert. She looks to me and her brows knit. "Children are evil, Tommaso," she sighs bitterly.

Stefano also appears distressed and helpless in the face of the expanding chaos. He and Elena exchange despairing glances. Raffaello leans toward Stefano and sings softly in his ear, the opening words of a sad and lovely song:

> I figli sai che son'?
> Son' piezz' u cor . . .
> (The children, you know what they are?
> They are the pieces of your heart.)

Stefano frowns at his wine and mutters, "They are the pieces of your balls!"

6. Six Months Later: Late One Night in Early April

Stefano is seated at a small table in the kitchen. Elena is standing behind him, doing dishes. The room is shadowy, and the meager light of a bare bulb is harsh. Stefano's eyes are like the eyes of a man suddenly gone blind, crazed and troubled. His son Pasquale has been hospitalized for swallowing poison.

"They tell us that he is bleeding internally. We never thought it was so serious." As he speaks, Stefano's fist clenches. "*Disgraziato* . . ." he whispers. Elena sighs and turns from her work. She pours herself some wine, but the wine is raw and she grimaces.

"I thought he was trying to get out of his chores, faking the whole thing. Who could know it was so serious? Oh Tommaso, when these things happen you lose all of your strength. You don't want to do anything well, to make anything . . . beautiful." Stefano says nothing. How small and weak he seems, with his head bowed and his shoulders fallen. His mouth is pulled tight with shame.

"Tell·me, Tommaso, what have I ever asked for? The only thing I've ever wanted of this life was to have all my children together here and gathered round me."

Elena asked if I would visit Pasquale the next morning. Would I bring his slippers to him, so that he wouldn't go about in the hallways barefooted.

"Don't forget them, Tommaso," her eyes were anxious and tense, "he needs his slippers."

chapter six

The Interpretation of Family Feeling

And so it was I entered the broken world,
To trace the visionary company of love . . .

Hart Crane

AT FIRST I found it challenging to record the myriad details of life in Stefano's household. But as time went on, the patterns revealed and repeated themselves. The shouting did not quiet down. The blows and kicks did not cease. The blindness and the bondage to the crudest emotions did not lessen, and I found myself increasingly exhausted after passing a few hours with them. Occasionally I felt constrained to leave them, and did not call upon them. They understood that on some level I was rejecting them and were offended. They had befriended me and shared their bread and wine with me. Why then did I avoid them?

Reliving the confused events of an afternoon as I wrote up my field notes became a wrenching chore. How could I record yet another exchange of insults, another bout of spitting, another discontinuous series of pecks and counterpecks? I began to block out sections of my notebook with the simple exclamation, "chaos!" which meant that the scene had flown out of perceptual control and I could no longer follow the flail of arms and fists, and the twisted, wincing faces, the curses, the grunts, and the cries.

79

The Interpretation of Family Feeling

The unconscious persecution of young Pasquale and his near martyrdom by suicide were especially harrowing to witness. As an outside observer and as a privileged guest of the family, I was in no position to interfere. Other relatives and friends had been told to mind their own business. Family life was private life in Naples, and family privacy was closely guarded and maintained. Stefano and Elena were concerned about the boy but they were doubly enraged with him because of the local publicity which his gesture incited. Upon returning from the hospital, Pasquale did not benefit from a happy homecoming. His abortive cry for help and compassion seemed only to have brought more wrath down upon him. His parents seemed to locate, in his many stumblings and awkward stances, all the minor and major forces which had impeded the progress of their own hopes and life-goals.

How they confounded me, Stefano and Elena and their children! Against such a backdrop of emotional carnage, how was I to understand the exasperating beauty of their closeness, their apparent need for one another, and the immediate sense of this group as a single, indivisible, though multicellular, organism? The constant flow of kisses and caresses attendant to the slaps and the kicks gave me the distinct impression of a unitary "colonial" personality. The notion of privacy did not exist for them, so long as they were together. For example, bathroom etiquettes were disconcertingly relaxed. An occupied bathroom was an open bathroom. Only Elena seemed to have been spared the dubious pleasure of a surprise visitor while engaged. The sleeping arrangements also enhanced this impression of an undivided social plasm. The parents slept on the matrimonial bed with the smaller boys, while Ciro, Gennaro, and Pasquale shared the bunk bed nearby. Nina slept beside them on her own bed. There was nothing fixed about where one slept. I recall one winter evening when Stefano retired early with Gennaro, and the two of them huddled close on the large bed, more like brothers than father and son. Sometimes, however, the children slept in the dining room, when their parents wanted to be alone.

When I befriended Ciro, Elena asked me if he and I would sleep together. To sleep beside another meant to trust and to care. My other friends at Fontana del Re also expected to sleep beside me as a token of friendship. It was a way of reassuring someone that you were there for them.

The family differed from other arenas of social life in the poor quarters because it was not a stage. Whatever a person might appear to be elsewhere, the family knew better. The secret weaknesses of the individual, the shame of sins long-hidden from the world, a grown man's cowering at night-borne terrors and fears—all this the family would assimilate and keep to itself. Also, the quiet strengths of a person, his or her special qualities of humor and tenderness, and all the unique talents to which the world was indifferent—these the family would recognize and applaud. Of course, if the talent were bogus the jeers would be merciless. If the honesty of the family was often cruel, it was also redemptive and sometimes therapeutic.

How typical or atypical is the family of Stefano and Elena and their children? How can we interpret their many contradictory actions? How can we understand, as an integrating or disintegrating whole, the agitated behavioral stream that carries this family along? Is this family to be dismissed as a freakish extreme, or can it be considered a variant of the normal? I cannot provide full answers to these questions. The psychoanalytically oriented research of Anne Parsons with lower-class Neapolitan families indicates that the aggression, conflict, and rivalry which are so much a part of Stefano's household are common features of daily life in the households of Naples.[1] With respect to Pasquale's unusual suicidal gesture, it is worth noting that many of the families at Fontana del Re, if examined closely, would reveal some glaring, atypical feature. A mother has run away. A father is in jail for stabbing a landlord. A son is homosexual. A sister has gone mad. A child is brain-damaged. The list of secret abnormalities could go on and on.

Human experience rarely accumulates in neat patterns and piles. People do not grow like crystals. Freud understood well that beneath the presentable surfaces of daily life the mind was not a tidy housekeeper. But whereas the middle and upper classes can at least afford to maintain appearances, among the poor the appearances are flimsy and fall apart easily, like fancy furniture bought on the installment plan. What Freud called the psychopathology of everyday life is exposed and dealt with as obscenity, humor, and cruelty in the kitchens and bedrooms of the poor.

The real world is very much with poor families. They live close to the sources of their own daily reality. Anger is violence. Love is touch. Food is security. Money is blood. The actions and reactions which churned about the table of Stefano and his children were weighted heavily with these values. Considered as a human group, responding to the stresses of poverty and class, Stefano's family is an archetypal unit confronting archetypal problems. It must organize and train for survival. It must instill in its members habits of selfishness and cunning, and yet it must demand self-sacrifice and a spirit of cooperation. It must teach violence and so it must breathe violence. Against the chantlike message of a world which tells the individual that he or she is worthless, the family must counter with an exaggerated message of personal power and strength. And within a civilization which deprives the lower-class individual of all opportunities for creative development and expression, the family must stand as the major and only creative enterprise of a lifetime, procreation being the sole reassurance of existential worth.

The relations of the family in poverty are overburdened and narrowed. As with combat units in battle, depending on the maturity and emotional skills of the leaders, heroism, efficiency, anarchy, or panic are all possible reactions to a crisis. But a core structure remains, with statuses and shared expectations. In the family of Stefano and Elena one can discern a structure of cooperation and authority that may be more or less standard in the poor quarters of Naples. Because of individual defects and weaknesses, one also discerns trends toward anarchy and panic that may not be common features of lower-class families. The core structure, however, is nuclear and based on the pooling of resources, while the statuses and expectations seem to revolve, for the most part, around the mother. But mother-centeredness does not necessarily bring with it a new Oedipal configuration, with Mom wearing the pants (as Anne Parsons has suggested)[2] nor need it presume a deep structure of matriarchy (as Ann Cornelisen has recently proposed).[3] The Neapolitan lower-class family intensifies and perhaps climaxes a general southern Italian pattern, different aspects of which have been identified by various researchers.[4] This family is mother-centered, father-ruled, and intensely nuclear.

Intense Nuclearity

Among poor rural folk in many parts of the world, the nuclear family can sometimes afford to grow another stem: one son remains on the land to plow and inherit, and to care for retired parents. This changeover has taken place in rural Italy when peasants are given more land.[5] But among the urban poor there is no such minuscule but productive property by which a parent stem can nourish the growth of another. In southern Italy, in city and agro-town alike, poverty has pressured toward nuclearity and flexibility with regard to the organization of domestic groups. In other words, people prefer to travel light when it comes to kinsmen.

This pattern contrasts with those of other poverty-stricken populations and cannot be taken as a universal tendency. Existing cultural conditions and differences in the overarching institutional framework mean that people will develop divergent ways of dealing with similar stresses. For example, the poor, urban black Americans studied by Carol Stack exhibit loosely knit and ill-defined nuclear households and rely on cooperating exchange networks of non-coresident kinfolk.[6] Here the weak nuclear pattern and the alternative adaptation of kin extension are related to a welfare system that discourages stable marriages. In lower-class Naples, in contrast to lower-class America, poor women are not penalized economically for marrying. Tightly structured and enduring nuclear units remain adaptive because of the division of labor, the mobility, and the redistribution of resources which they provide. Poverty is a limiting factor on the size of the domestic group. Mafia-style clans are a bourgeois luxury which the poor people of Fontana del Re would be very hard-pressed to maintain.

At Fontana del Re, broken nuclear units were patched up or otherwise compensated for, but they were not fitted into a wider extended pattern. Older women in particular cared for the children of their deceased (or in one case, runaway) daughters, but they demanded financial help from the fathers and room and board money from the older grandchildren. The emphasis on nuclearity creates tension between the generations, as the family one grew up in becomes gradually less important than the family one raises children in. Neapolitan parents like to recite, within earshot of their children, a cynical proverb that states: "One mother can take care of one hundred children, but one hundred children cannot take care of one mother." The structural regularity beneath the complaint has less to do with filial ingratitude than with the overwhelming demands and pressures which grown-up children face when trying to maintain nuclear families of their own.

Beyond the nuclear unit, which pools the incomes and labor of mother, father, and all able-bodied, unmarried children, no clear-cut set of expectations or social procedures has evolved in relation to other kinsmen. This lack of clarity may be adaptive. If poverty has imposed limitations on the size of the domestic group, it has also encouraged flexibility toward the outlying network of relatives, or *parentela*. Non-nuclear kin are viewed opportunistically, either as kinsmen obligated to help you or as friends, coincidentally related, whom one should feel free to turn away, although not without profuse explanations and excuses. In effect, this ambiguity allows people to play both sides of the fence. This utilitarian, maximizing stance toward anyone outside the nuclear family has led Edward Banfield to characterize southern Italians as "amoral familists." But Banfield's concept, in addition to being causally lopsided, conveys a false image of complete nuclear introversion.[7] At Fontana del Re, visiting and commensality were commonplace among relatives. One's relatives (non-coresident siblings, aunts, uncles, cousins, etc.) were invariably sentimentalized publicly and scorned in private. The exuberance of the praise and the vehemence of the curses usually depended on where the individual stood in the accounting of reciprocities which every person at Fontana del Re kept like a ledger in the forefront of his mind.

According to Stefano and Elena (as recounted in scene 4 in the preceding chapter), any kinsman outside the immediate domestic group, including an older parent, could no more be relied upon for help in a crisis than a casual friend. But although help was never to be taken for granted, forms of cooperation and aid did exist among kinsmen, especially if such cooperation and aid were mutually beneficial. Stefano, for example, cooperated economically with two brothers who resided in other districts. They exchanged labor and pooled trucks on jointly undertaken moving jobs. But other siblings residing nearby were rarely seen. When I was cheated by a plumber who overcharged me for a fixture, Elena tried to console me by telling of her cousin who was a carpenter and had installed her kitchen cabinets. Because she was his relative, he cheated her for only half of what he would have taken from a stranger. When I expressed indignant surprise, she scoffed at my naiveté.

Stefano and Elena asserted that, in times of severe hardship, they neither asked for nor received help from relatives. But the bitterness with which they made these assertions betrayed a sense of disappointment and abandonment, and implied a deep-seated ambivalence toward this category of kin outside the household, including parents and siblings. In the slums of Naples, the family intimacies and loyalties of youth are weakened by the establishment of a new procreative unit, and those whom one formerly leaned upon, trusted, and loved are propelled outward into the uncertain and unregulated frontier zone which exists between the household and the community.

Mother-Centeredness
and the Question of Matriarchy

If an academic sociologist had conducted a study of blue-collar family life in an American factory town in 1943, and had somehow not known that there was a war going on, he might have concluded that the average American working-class family was matrifocal since fathers were often absent and mothers were working in typically male occupations. Poverty is certainly as powerful a reagent of social relationships as is warfare, but its effects on the way people relate to one another are not always seen for what they are: as difficult adjustments to unpleasant circumstances which everyone hopes will soon cease to exist.

The Neapolitan lower-class family is neither matrifocal nor matriarchal, because the mother is not a provider or a power-holder who supercedes the father. She may share power with him and she may have more prestige. She is the living center of a tight-bonded human group, but she is not the boss. For this reason, I prefer the term "mother-centered" to describe the pattern under discussion here.

The points of difference between mother-centered families and matrifocal ones are subtle and easily confounded. In the slums of Naples the role of the mother is subject to a great deal of cultural elaboration, but this elaboration applies only to her undisputed monopoly over child care and the flow of family feeling. In genuine matrifocal systems, as Nancy Tanner has indicated, the mother is a legitimate economic and ritual actor as well and is fully accepted as the equal of any male in these domains.[8]

The emotional centrality of the mother in the households of the poor is often seen as being related to the economic degradation of men. In the conventional view,

87

strong and resourceful women maintain their families while their demoralized husbands hang about on street-corners. This image does not reflect the realities of economic life among the poor of Naples. Men are not so much unemployed as temporarily employed, and both sexes are socialized to be strong and resourceful. Moreover, the idea of a single breadwinner doing all the work and shouldering all financial responsibilities is countered by the importance attached to the labor and cash contributions of children. Mother-centeredness is not the result of male degradation and breakdown, but rather flows naturally from the radial and redistributive patterning of the family economy.

Diverse resources are donated to the mother. These "donations" are often solicited from recalcitrant children by the father, for the mother. The mother then converts and redistributes these resources in the form of what for the poor is the most highly valued resource of all, palatable food. As a redistributor the mother accumulates prestige but, as in other redistributive arrangements, she is often left with less than anybody else, though she works harder. She is a "big woman," admired, important, and indispensable, but she does not acquire real power. Stefano and his sons are economically essential. Stefano is a good provider, but this fact in no way challenges Elena's affective centrality in the household. The mother is the one who feeds people and, as Anne Parsons also noted, she feeds them continuously;[9] this is the organizing activity of her day. I once asked Elena to tell me about her daily round of chores. She brought me up to midday before Robertino drew her away:

"I get up first, every day at seven. I wake Stefano. I make coffee for him. Then while he gets ready for work, I have to get everybody's clothes pressed and ready for the day. He's off to work. Next I make the *caffe-latte* for Gennaro, and Ciro, and Pasquale. I wake them and serve them. And they're off to work. Now the little ones have to be sent off to school, so I make them a *zuppa di latte* (milk soup) with bread and get them out of bed and serve them. And after they're dressed and off, I give Robertino his bottle of warmed milk, and dress him and leave him to play. My husband and my sons will be arriving toward mid-day from their jobs and the kids will be home from school, so I've got to get their lunches ready. The stuffed sandwiches have to be prepared and this takes up the rest of the morning."

The main meal of the day was supper and we hadn't come near it yet.

Elena is at the center because she controls and distributes the twin sources of human vitality, food and love. Theoretically, ideally, she bestows her affections like her food, unconditionally and equally. Unlike Stefano, who is free to choose and announce favorites, Elena is anxious to preserve at least the façade of emotional democracy ("All of my children are bravo!").

Unlike the Mediterraneans, the Hindus wisely portray their mother goddess, Kali, in two aspects, the one nurturant and soft, the other terrible and cruel. Her power to love is matched only by her power to destroy. Elena reveals this same dual aspect in her relations with her children. She is their fierce lover and defender, and they look to her and celebrate her as such, in keeping with the Neapolitan ideal. In many ways, she does not disappoint. She wards off the evils of hunger, cold, and dirt, providing all with the maternal gifts of carefully cooked food, warmth, and cleanliness. In the uncertain social arenas beyond the home, Elena stands ready to defend her children against

89

the petty defeats of street-squabbles and she offers countervailing force to any adult who might abuse them (recall her attack on Raffaello in scene 3). Against the alien powers of schoolteachers, policemen, and psychologists, she can at least exercise her right to vocal objection. I recall her furious verbal battle with a policeman over her child's right to cool himself in a public fountain, and the way in which she once intimidated a child psychologist who wanted to classify her delinquent son, Ciro, as "psychoneurotic." "My son isn't crazy!" She shook her fist at the man and protested. "He's a nervous boy. He flies off the handle easily. But he's no nut!"

Elena sought no special recognition for her expenditures of energy and care. By contrast, Stefano was always reminding his children of how many sacrifices he had made for them. He compared himself with other fathers, hoping to rise in the estimation of his children, but Stefano was always second to Elena, and sometimes even third in the family popularity ratings.

When I was introduced to lower-class people in Naples, to old men or to young children, a very common first question to me was "C'è l'hai la Mamma? C'è l'hai?" Always the first concern, the first empathetic projection, was, "Do you have your mother?" and then, "How do you manage without her?" No other kin relation was ever mentioned, never the parents or the father, only the mother. And Elena reported that when her mother died, she lost contact with her emigrant brother as well, because the critical tie between them was now severed (see scene 4).

"Of fathers, how many there are, but of mothers, there is only one." Invoking this popular proverb, half in jest, Ciro (in scene 5) alluded to the biogrammatic and historically determined relation between structure and sentiment in lower-class Naples, with regard to parents and children. Whereas maternity is verifiable, paternity is

90

not. Whereas mothers tend to remain close to home, fathers go out to work, often to foreign lands. In any case, the presence of fathers is not to be relied on as part of the natural order of things. Mother love, on the other hand, is seen as a fixed certainty. Barring her death, she is simply there, like the Madonna in the niche. One of the hit songs of the season when I was in Naples was "Mamma, Addo Sta?" (Mamma, where is she?), a melodramatic ballad which tells the story of a sailor who returns home to be greeted by everyone except the one for whom he has reserved his deepest yearning.

The love of fathers is achieved. Mother love is ascribed. Fathers do not have inalienable claims on the affections of their children. But this does not mean that the father is weak in lower-class Naples, as Parsons suggests. Perhaps because of his affective distance, the emotional division of labor delegates the severest disciplinary responsibilities to him. A mother might strike her children brutally and at will, but her threats and blows are not feared as are those of the father. If Elena wanted a child beaten, she could do it herself, but if Stefano were present, she could motion to him and he would carry out the sentence. If he wanted to strike a child, he did so without asking and often to excess. The tyranny of the fathers of Naples is part of the lore of children. They compare their scars. They relate their adventures in hospital.

Ann Cornelisen, in concluding her sharp-etched series of portraits on the harsh lives of Italian women in Lucania, declares the society of southern Italy to be organized on a matriarchal and not, as is commonly supposed, a patriarchal pattern.[10] (Anne Parsons derives similar conclusions from her psychological investigations.) In an economy where men must either migrate to find work or spend half their lives waiting in piazzas for it, women perform many of the vital tasks of society. In many male-dominated societies where the division of labor places a heavy burden on women, the reigning ideology of male supremacy may not reflect day-to-day realities. But the fact that any category of persons (whether stratificational, sexual, racial, or ethnic) holds a society together, providing the energy for its effective continuance, is not in itself grounds for concluding that such a group is politically superordinate; ie., that it possesses positive power, the power to compel, as opposed to merely negative power, the power to withdraw, as in a strike. I agree with Cornelisen that the conventional ideology of male supremacy is insufficient to explain the facts of life in southern Italy, but I think she is oversimplifying the human realities which she has described with such uncompromising and passionate honesty.

In Naples, as in Lucania, women were not the docile wives of Italian myth. (I have already pointed to the prestige accruing to them as redistributors, as "big women.") They did not stand by silently, a few paces behind their husbands, ready unconditionally to serve. They were not shut away from the world, in the isolated darkness of their homes. They were defiant women, ready to challenge any man's decisions if they judged them unwise. Elena never hesitated to tell her husband outright to shut up. She disagreed with him openly on politics and religion. If he annoyed her, she might take a shoe to him as impulsively as to anyone else. Nor was she always confined to the home. In hard times she had toiled in artificial flower sweatshops, and she had sold cigarettes. Occasionally, in the past, she had lent money out at interest to neighbors. (Stefano told me that these small loans paid for an occasional luxury for him. "She earns the interest and I eat it.") Elena was the resident consumer expert. But when Stefano earns enough, and the children contribute, Elena does not work. Her proper place is in the home.

In nondomestic arenas, Elena beats up arrogant waiters and threatens thin-lipped bureaucrats more effectively than her easy-going husband. But then, Stefano was able to maintain a nice-guy image only because his wife did most of the social dirty work of defending and quarreling. Actually, they worked together in the neighborhood as a Janus-faced social unit. He could push for local popularity, prestige, and respect, "for myself and my children," while she could argue about the price of bread and fish and deliver insults and threaten revenge when the need arose. Her bellowing voice and stomping gait evoked terror at home and abroad. Gossips and bullies alike would have to reckon with her. By anyone's standards she was a formidable woman. But whatever power she had derived solely from her position as a wife and mother. The great bulk of her considerable energies were focused on the responsibilities which these roles, and especially the maternal role, entailed. When Elena's older brother came to visit, she expressed fear that he would slap her if he saw her smoking.

The women of southern Italy are powerful only in the sense that they perform "powerfully" the innumerable tasks and chores which men and children set for them. Women as wives are extolled, and women as mothers are deified, but women as women do not count for much in southern Italy. Men refer to them, as they pass in the street, synecdochically—a part of the body suffices to identify any female who is not immediately recognizable as a wife or mother.

Male values go unchallenged by the poor women of Naples. Mothers teach domesticity and toughness to their daughters. They teach aggression, predation, and phallic pride to their sons. (I have seen housewives on the streets of Naples shaking and boasting about the penises of their baby boys.) Among the lower classes in Naples, I think there is a trend toward uniformity of temperament between the sexes. But the trend is definitely in the direction of behaviors traditionally associated with the male. (Recalling Margaret Mead's classic research, the Neapolitans approach more closely the Mundugumor pattern where both sexes were aggressive and given to violence.[11]) In street battles, when angered, housewives assume the alter-ego of the male, and daily shout, with masculine ferocity, "Non ce rompere cazz' a me!" (literally, Don't bust my prick!). True, the traditionally accepted image of the southern Italian woman is a false projection, and true, the maternal role is at the center of the family circle; but the power of the male, and the idea of the power adhering to things male, continues to suffuse a culture whose masters have always been sons and lovers and likewise tyrants first, and only secondly husbands and fathers.

Favoritism and Rivalry

Although Elena guarantees some critical minimum of nurturance to all, she doles out her affections in different quantities and at different times. She consistently overprotects one child, while neglecting or abusing others. Robertino receives too much mothering while Pasquale receives too little. It may be that age is a factor here, that Elena dotes over her young, only to abandon them when they reach a certain age. Extreme favoritism toward Robertino was often rationalized on the basis of his age. Also, his young age exempted him from economic pressures and tensions, which certainly influenced family psychodynamics. Gennaro is well-loved, his father tells us, because he brings home the largest paycheck (see scene 1 in the last chapter). Ciro is beaten when he refuses to work. But Pasquale, the object of general abuse, works at a job and at home. The emotional spectrum does not match up simply with the family budget.

One gives love as one has learned to receive it. Elena reports (in scene 4) that her own mother cultivated favorites and that she was not one of them. Here, then, is a possibly neurotic and possibly cultural pattern in process of transmission from one generation to another. But why neurotic and how cultural? The first question relates to clinical judgments about what is good for people; the second relates to people's own judgments about what is good for them. Since Stefano and Elena were criticized by their relatives and friends for their treatment of Pasquale, since they were evasive and defensive about him, and since favoritism was shunned in the family of Michele and Angela, I do not think that extreme child favoritism is a built-in normative feature of Neapolitan lower-class life. But favoritism is a theme which echoes through the local social system of the poor quarters. If the behavior of Stefano and Elena is not cultural, neither is it exceptional. It draws on psychodynamic currents that are not idiosyncratic.

For example, when little Giuseppe was exhorted to choose between myself and Raffaello (in scene 3), Raffaello participated as a willing contestant. He saw nothing amiss. Stefano and Elena (in scene 5) clearly set up the momentous question of stringbeans versus tomatoes as a mock drama that would create yet another occasion for the selection of a favorite and the reaffirmation of the primacy of the maternal-filial dyad. From his exalted position, the family favorite Robertino was often asked to choose favorites. His favor was actively courted by siblings with precarious positions in the family, especially Ciro. At Fontana del Re, I was repeatedly asked to select and publicly announce my favorite acquaintance or friend. When I refused, my sincerity was compromised and my friendship devalued.

95

In Brecht's dramatization of the lumpenproletarian view of the world, *Mother Courage*, he retells the parable of St. Martin's famous cloak: "And he gave this fellow half his cloak to wear; so both of them fell down and froze."[12] Among poor folk the image of limited good is a rational assessment of the predicament of man in society, and it intrudes upon all domains of behavior, emotional as well as economic.[13] To favor one person is to deny another, but it is to favor the one. It permits one person to luxuriate, however briefly, in the exclusive love of another. It celebrates the single dyadic union and extolls the benefits of mutually intense as opposed to more diffuse, democratic, and therefore diluted personal commitments. Finally, in a social stratum where large families have been the rule for centuries, is it any wonder that people should place a high value on special attention, that they should wish to be singled out and chosen, and loved in isolation, and that this wish to love and be loved as such should express itself in their social rituals and in the demands, distortions, and pressures of intimate family life?

Certainly a great deal of the strife and violence which raged in Stefano's household can be attributed to the bitterness engendered by competition for the leftovers of parental affection after Rob had taken the lion's share. Yet none of Stefano's children exhibited denial symptoms, that cool, flat indifference to others so often manifest in emotionally starved children. As a group, as a category, *i figli*, they were cared for and protected, but they were also resented for the burdens they imposed. They were all loved, but some were loved more and some were loved less. The result was an emotional minefield, with winners and losers constantly battling and wounding one another (with occasional attempts to administer first aid). When the tension rose to intolerable levels, a scapegoat, Pasquale, was selected to serve as the family shock absorber.[14] By finally focusing intense hostility against one child, the parents could more effectively express their sense of indentured bondage to all their children. Siblings could concentrate and release their pent-up jealousies on a legitimatized object, with impunity. But this particular scapegoat rebelled in such a way as to publicly dramatize his persecution. Nevertheless, by risking self-destruction as opposed to destruction by others, the boy only revealed the real dimensions of the trap which enclosed him.

In the family of Stefano and Elena, parental immaturity translated into sibling rivalry, insecurity, and, possibly, chronic immaturity in later life. I have no way of knowing to what extent these patterns are prevalent in other poor families. In the first family referred to, the mother had rejected and scapegoated her runaway sons as part of a more general withdrawal from the demands of the maternal role. In the second case, Angela and Michele were devoted to their children but unstable in their relationship with each other. In the family of Stefano and Elena, the fault lines were not conjugal but parental-filial and fraternal. Admittedly this data is insufficient, but it indicates a variety of emotional processes at work in poor families (albeit on a nuclear, "matricentric," and male-supremacist base). Sweeping generalizations about social pathology are inappropriate here.

Socialization: Indulgence and Violence

The pattern of oscillation between indulgence and violence was not unique at Fontana del Re, or in other poor districts. For example, the family of Luciano (a junk-collec-

tor colleague of Stefano's) was less violent but just as raucous. Group excursions to the beach with these two families were memorable.

In contrast to Luciano's yellowed, fish-skeleton looks,
his wife Maddalena was round and vigorous. When her
children annoyed her, she never hesitated to bat them
about. Her attentions were focused on her youngest child,
a cherubic one-year-old girl. Maddalena fondled, ca-
ressed, and fed this child continually. When she changed
her diaper, she leant down close to coo and giggle softly.
She patted her and pinched her lightly. She kissed her
mouth, abdomen, and genitals. At the same time, she
could be ruthless with her other children. Her nine-year-
old daughter received one slap after another for assorted
offenses. (This child was filthy. Her feet were covered with
sores.) When her oldest child, an eleven-year-old boy, cut
himself on a shell and began to cry, Maddalena only
laughed at his distress. When I rose to assist him, she
shouted, "My son is a *pecora* [sheep, or sissy]. Leave him
alone." He was an overweight boy with reddish hair and a
gentle manner, but he was not effeminate.

At Fontana del Re, I once saw an old woman chase her
grandson in the street. The boy ran ahead of her and then
turned to face her, brandishing a beer bottle. He smashed
the bottle against a stone wall and mocked the old woman
with the jagged, glinting edges. After the inevitable crowd
had gathered and argued and tempers had calmed, I
watched the boy as he swaggered away from the scene.
No punishment and no reprimand had been issued for the
makeshift weapon. No one ever thought he would use it,
but neither did anyone question his right to fashion and
wield it. At Fontana del Re, children, especially male children, were encouraged to be aggressive and even dangerous, as the situation warranted. A child who did not turn

98

out this way was scoffed at, by his parents as much as by anyone else, as a "pecora."

Among certain hunting groups, patterns of neuromuscular coordination are taught at an early age to boys. Older males cradle and rock and play with a male child in ways that will stretch some muscles and not others. Habits of mind appropriate to the hunt are developed concurrently.[15] In Naples, among the lower classes, older males engaged in a kind of play activity with male children whose purpose seems to be to develop a neuromuscular and psychological readiness for frenetic violence.

Vincenzo was a jack of all trades, recently turned pimp. One day, as I passed him in the street, he invited me to admire his two-year-old son. He was proud of the boy and very affectionate with him. Because he was separated from his wife, he saw the child only infrequently. Vincenzo expressed his feeling for the boy through gestures which were standard elements in the local grammar of paternal male affection.

The child wore a soiled, torn gown. His light skin was marred by blemishes and impetigo sores. His blonde hair was crew-cut, accentuating the forehead and magnifying the clear, pale blue eyes. Vincenzo tickled him and tossed him into the air, eliciting peals of laughter. With a fanlike flurry of movements, he waved his hands in the child's face and proceeded to slap him, quickly and lightly, until the boy became confused and seemed on the brink of tears. Then he tossed him again, and squeezed him close, and finally resumed the slapping game. An enormous sac-bellied woman arrived to fetch the child. The baby cried, "Babbo, Babbo," as she carried him off. Vincenzo was somber.

A playful exchange of slaps instructs a boy in aggression and a stance of self-defense. But this adaptive fusion

99

of violence with love becomes sinister when affection turns to anger or rage. Two young male friends of mine at Fontana del Re once compared their scars for my benefit. Most of these derived from beatings administered by parents. Pepe, pointing to a whitish patch of skin on his leg, told how his father had once bounced him on the pavement like a soccer ball. Parting his hair to reveal a section of scalp, he recalled how his mother had taken an iron rod, years before, and split open his head (his father then beat her, took twenty thousand lire, and went off to a whore). Gennaro's mother had given him a blow on the head with a cast-iron pot. When the blood bubbled up and flowed out from his hair, she rushed him to the hospital.

I asked them if their parents had ever repented these actions. Gennaro replied, "No, and if they ever do they certainly wouldn't show it." Pepe reported that he once saw his father weep with remorse for a deep slash he had given him with a stick. I then asked them if they would beat their own children in the same way. Pepe said, "Yes, if they deserved it I would beat them, but then, I'm *nervoso* anyway. When I get angry, I can't stop, can't help myself. So I know I'll beat them. I threw my little brother down the stairs the other day because he dropped a glass of milk!" After some reflection, Gennaro said he too had an uncontrollable temper, but he would not beat his children *a sangue* (to blood) because the scars were ugly reminders to parents later.

On a summer day at Fontana del Re, from my balcony I watch the babies and children scattered about, crawling and playing on the cobblestones below. They play in the dirt. The male babies are naked. They scramble out of the way of the cars which zoom in and out of the compound. If any of the children chances upon a piece of rope, or a stick, or a section of chain, he will beat a companion or a wall with it, whichever is closest. They fight amongst themselves and sometimes precipitate noisy battles between their mothers and grandmothers. One child has some matches. He sets fire to a stack of newspapers and watches them burn. Adults look on from a distance but do not interfere. These children are loud. They are never shy or subdued. They will shout back at any angered adult, "Bocchinatto" (cocksucker). They know that for this they will not be punished. In fact, they have learned that, in subtle ways, intractability is praised. Two of the children call to me, and I wave down at them. One of them tosses an apple core at me. Another is aiming a rough-hewn slingshot. The pebble narrowly misses my head. The boy's father passes. He has witnessed the near miss. He greets me warmly, and lifts the child to his arms, kissing him tenderly on the mouth.

The poor families of Naples teach their children early about the essential human joys. The humanity of the dependent babe is nurtured in a permissive atmosphere of tactile and nutritive warmth. Positive social interactions are charged with spontaneous sensual energy, at once intense and relaxed.

But how soon must the young child be impressed and taught how to survive in a social system that seeks only to hunt his life force down, and make it captive to engines of accumulation which are indifferent to his needs. How soon will he note, and himself begin to suffer, the devastation of spirit which the facts of deprivation and inequality have wrought in the locale of his known world.

In a family like Stefano's the emerging self does not take final shape in a creative dialogue of give and take with others but instead is forced to struggle for ascendancy in a violent competitive arena. To what extent are such families training grounds for the realities of life on the street and at the bottom of the wider world? I do not think that marking

101

a child for emotional death, as Pasquale was marked, prepares him for anything beyond a concentration camp, but encouraging him to be fierce, to strike quickly and without hesitation, and to push and lever his way to a position of physical or emotional advantage does prepare him in critical ways for survival in a world founded on the crude protocols of brute force. The brutality of the poor is learned. It imitates the brutality of class.

chapter seven

The Triumvirate of Want

At the very best, he who is branded by affliction will keep only half his soul.

Simone Weil

THE SMALLEST CHILDREN at Fontana del Re, whenever they approached me, came forward with palms extended, begging for small change. It was automatic with them, this mechanical extension of the palm, as though someone had trained them to it. They hardly saw me as they recited their requests, and they rarely insisted if I refused. Begging was as natural to them as smiling.

Poor people care about money to the point of obsession. But with the poor, money is for spending. It is for quick conversion into life. Since money and life are so closely interconnected in their minds, they do not fetishize money in the capitalist mode but rather crave it as something they have missed. Indeed, this craving for money is never more marked than in the slums. There, money is survival, for the organism as for the spirit, and survival is the uneasy peace toward which men must strive.

One afternoon I heard the hoarse loud voice of young Ciro calling me to my balcony. Rising to greet him, I saw him in the midst of some other youths. They huddled around him as though he were guarding something rare and alive. Upon seeing me, he thrust his arms up toward me to exhibit his treasure. He fingered, in his large grimy hands, a few tattered bills. "I robbed them, Tommaso!" he whispered, and his face broke into a smile that was like a leer.

Food and money and love formed a terrible and corruptive triumvirate of want at Fontana del Re. Workers and thieves, housewives and whores—all bowed alike to the power of these masters. In empathy or else in anger, each had to recognize a bit of himself in the pose of the other.

St. Francis was wise to consecrate poverty and humility together. Being broke is an intolerable condition, analogous to sensory deprivation. It makes a man turn away from his children. It cuts him off from the good company of his friends. He cannot give, and is ashamed to take what is offered. Should he take then what is not offered? The inability to buy a caffè for oneself or to offer it to someone else can set a fire of bitterness growing within a man, forcing him to choices and decisions which may alter irrevocably his image of himself and the world. If a thief had a windfall at Fontana del Re, he would offer drinks and pastries to the others and solemnly watch them consume his gifts. But beneath the conviviality everyone was grim.

Food and money and love—no one could have all three at Fontana del Re. Food, of course, was the first fury before whom they kneeled. I saw no starvation in the year I was there. But the people were divided on money and love, and whichever they chose to serve, they would be hounded to their deaths by the one they denied.

An Infamous History

The stones of Fontana del Re give off the dank odor of centuries. They have witnessed the rise and decline of Spanish viceroys and Bourbon kings, and have absorbed the shocks of countless rampaging mobs. Masaniello, the ill-fated fisherman-liberator, may have trod these lanes. Perhaps Garibaldi's regiments paused here for a drink of wine. Here the Nazi troops marched, and the fatal American bombs fell nearby. Still the buildings endure, hollowed stone cavernlike shells, hosting yet another generation; mute testimonials to a past dominated by foreign conquerors and local scoundrels and dreamers who thought that dreams were sufficient to put right the terrible imbalance of the world.

The Neapolitan economy is built upon the ruined foundations of this past and bears the stigmata of an infamous history. Her industries remain underdeveloped. They reflect the needs, not of a teeming mass market, but of a bygone aristocracy. In preindustrial Naples the arsenal produced guns, while her great workshops unfurled endless shimmering rolls of silk. Against this backdrop of rifles and luxuriant cloth, how often the people rioted for their bread! How often they succumbed to the merciless time-keeping of the cholera!

Fernand Braudel describes sixteenth-century Naples as "a monumental parasite," whose great wealth and population—unrivaled in Europe and surpassed only by Constantinople in the Mediterranean—derived from the Faustian pact she had made with the new territorial state. The absolutist Spanish state concentrated its managerial personnel and its Italian wealth in the Kingdom of the Two Sicilies and the city grew, like an irresponsible, overfed child, oblivious of the future and incapable of self-support. "Naples," Braudel writes, "was excessive in every respect . . . the most astonishing, most fantastically picaresque city in the world."[1]

The Mediterranean, which had been in antiquity a Roman lake and mother sea to so many civilizations, became a backwater as Northern Europe prospered and capi-

105

talism matured on the profits of the Atlantic trading. As the Renaissance expired and as Spanish power declined, Naples lost her preeminence as a major world capital. With the unification of Italy in the nineteenth century, she also lost her place as capital of the Kingdom of the Two Sicilies and became politically peripheral and economically subordinate to northern power emanating from Milan and Rome. But if history has stripped Naples of her former glories, it has allowed the city to retain her notoriety as a center of overpopulation and squalor.

More babies die in Naples than in any other city in Europe. The infant mortality rate is 71 per 1000 births.[2] In Naples, as many as five thousand human habitations are no more than caves, shanties, and huts. Two of the largest wards of the city have the highest population density in Europe, and a full 70 percent of all families live in dwellings of one or two rooms, with 2.5 to 3 persons per room. One-third of all Neapolitan families still reside in the one-room ground-floor dwellings known as *bassi*.[3] Life in an old basso might strike an outsider as romantic, but more often than not these dwellings are damp, poorly lit, cramped, and in direct contact with traffic-congested streets. Journalists refer to Naples as "the Calcutta of Europe," and Romans make racist jokes about the African capital to the south. But both recognize in their ways, of hyperbole or bias, a fundamental reality—Naples forms part of the Third World.

Naples is the third largest city in the nation, after Rome and Milan, with an officially registered population of 1,220,000. Whereas in Milan 30.6 percent of the population works in the industrial sector, in Naples only 8.8 percent of the total population can be classified as industrially employed.[4] Moreover, the meaning of the word "industrial" in Naples is significantly different from what it is in Milan. If Percy Allum's descriptive analysis of the Neapolitan economy as being dualistic is accurate, the industrial sector has changed only superficially over the past five hundred years:

It consists of a small number of highly mechanised factories and a myriad of tiny handicraft shops and is marked by the almost total absence of medium-sized firms. In fact, almost 90% of the so-called industrial undertakings employ less than five persons while medium-sized concerns (100–1,000 employees) account for exactly 0.4% of the industrial labour force. So the contrast is between the mammoth Italsider steel works at Bagnoli which has a 6,000 strong highly paid work force . . . and the tiny artisan shop with its family structure and its little-developed division of labour dependent on local needs and congenitally insecure. [5]

Limited industrialization, then, has laid the basis for the emergence of a germinal working proletariat, with an identity and problems of its own. But approximately 60 percent of the active population of the city is classified in the census data as belonging to the "service" sector of the economy. As the sociologist Antonio Vitiello has pointed out, such a blanket classification tells us very little about the "tertiary occupations of the underproletariat."[6] Most Neapolitans belong to an underclass that does not work in big factories and offices. The majority remain trapped in the rubble of five centuries of silent class warfare and foreign or northern domination. Somehow they manage to find their way through the debris. The word they use for this special skill is *arrangiarsi,* the art of arranging whatever bits and fragments of money-yielding activity they can find into a successful strategy of survival.

Making Ends Meet at Fontana del Re

Approximately 200 people lived at Fontana del Re in 32 households. Precise data was difficult to obtain since formal census-style inquiries renewed old suspicions about

the anthropologist as tax agent. People were under-
standably reluctant to reveal all the facts about how they
made a living. Moreover, for many persons the concept of
a single occupation had very little practical meaning.

Enzo the sailor, for example, worked on a cruise ship
a few months out of the year, but at other times he was a
waiter or a peddler of stolen clothes. Gabriele the wid-
ower broke up metallic junk with the help of his four children, but he also ran a small sundries store in the district
and at night served as the taxi-chauffeur for the prostitutes
of a nearby brothel. He even managed to pick up a few
extra lire selling cosmetics and clothing to the whores on
their way home. The Neapolitan economy is like Huxley's
barrel of apples; every available niche has been filled.

Some people held only one job at Fontana del Re—
servants and bartenders, dockworkers, sanitationmen, and
a few artisans. One young man made his living grooming
the poodles of the rich. But there were also the jacks-of-
all-trades and the full-time rogues, who hung about in the
main piazzas to guide a lonely sailor to just the right night-
club or sell him a gold watch at a price so low he'd be a
fool to refuse. There were a few smugglers at Fontana del
Re, and more than a few burglars, pickpockets, and purse-
snatchers. Many of these combined their criminal activities
with part-time legitimate work, usually in house or mechanical repairs. There were flower vendors and beggars,
and there were the old women who collected their small
pensions and earned the rest selling contraband cigarettes, and condoms, and greasy sandwiches and beer,
and wine so bad it burned a hole through your gut. Even
the children earned their keep, laboring in small workshops after school or instead of school. Stefano's daughter
Nina, age ten, seemed happy enough to earn her eight
dollars a week working thirty hours after school in a small
pocketbook workshop. Pepe, the eleven-year-old son of a
local cobbler, worked in a television repair shop. He was

glad to be learning a trade, but his face and his chest were marked with the burn-scars left by exploding tubes. It was his task to test the defectives. On the main avenue near Fontana del Re some of the younger boys of the district, aged seven and eight, could be seen every morning scurrying about between the parked cars, prying the trunks open in an instant to make off with whatever they could carry. Other boys belonged to the youthful army of the *portacaffè*, who carried small trays of espresso to the offices and shops of the city. Stefano's son Pasquale, for example, worked for a large cafe in the midtown business district. He earned approximately ten dollars a week for thirty hours of work, minus the two hundred lire which his boss deducted weekly for breakage, even if nothing broke.

Since many of the people of Fontana del Re were self-employed, they were painfully vulnerable to the caprices of a recessive economy. A winter's prosperity could turn suddenly to a springtime of penury. Even though the familiar symptoms of poverty might temporarily disappear, the chronic insecurity which is at the heart of the condition remained, to undermine the foundations of community and to gnaw at the individual's peace of mind. I remember the economic situation of my friend Michele, the dressmaker, who did not reside at Fontana del Re but whose situation was typical of the artisans of Naples.

When I first met him in April of 1974, Michele was earning well, receiving enough orders for dresses to keep himself and his wife-assistant, Angela, busy in their workshop living room from seven to seven, six days a week. Michele and Angela set their table well, with meat as a frequent second course. When Angela, who was pregnant, began to suffer from fatigue, Michele arranged for her and their ailing two-year-old son to spend a month during the summer at an inexpensive beach cottage.

In April of 1975, Michele and Angela had another

child, but orders for dresses dropped off inexplicably and Michele was idle for weeks on end. When an emergency fund of two hundred dollars disappeared mysteriously, Michele and Angela became suspicious of close friends. Angela was exhausted and depressed, overburdened by the demands of a frail and sickly infant and a three-year-old son. All trace of meat vanished from their table. When the newborn fell ill with a virus and nearly died, Michele began to wonder—To which nation should he migrate? To what city? Would he find work in his trade? Should he bring his family? When? Now or later? Would things in Naples ever improve?

In 1974–1975 the streets of Naples yielded up to my friend Stefano, the junkman, a bounty of cardboard and discarded washing machines, water heaters, and stoves. Stefano sold the cardboard for recycling and meticulously disassembled the seemingly indestructible metal paraphernalia to sell the parts and the scrap. But Naples, though full of junk, is no Eden for junk collectors. Too many junkmen compete with one another and the sanitation department for the leavings of the middle classes. To supplement an uneven income, Stefano used his small truck to do moving jobs as well. In this he cooperated with two brothers who owned small trucks of their own. Stefano preferred the heavy loading and transport work to scavenging for junk, but fell back on scavenging during the frequent intervals between moving jobs. His only capital was his small wheelbarrow-shaped truck. For labor, he relied on his children and his own powerful, callused back. Sometimes at his table Elena would fill my glass and intone solemnly, "This wine is my husband's blood, Tommaso. We don't let just anyone drink it!"

That year Stefano did not earn enough to dress well or to save, yet he and his family ate well, and this gave him a great sense of satisfaction and well-being. But Stefano was haunted by memories of a hungrier past. Perhaps this was why he chose to spend the greater part of his earnings on good, abundant food. He and Elena and their oldest son ate quickly and to excess, as if they had known hunger and assumed they would know it again. His younger children ate at a slower pace and often left food on their plates.

Stefano took bitter pleasure in recounting time after time, to me and to his children, his recollections of hard times past. He told of a time ten years before, when he and his wife were reduced to eating bread and coffee on Christmas Day, while the children made the most of what the nuns provided. No one offered to help, neither brother nor friend. For the following Easter the meal was better. The Signora had found a more generous order of nuns.

In those days Stefano was a cobbler in a small shoe factory. The wages were low, and he was subject to recurrent periods of unemployment. Stefano is happier as a junkman. He brings in more money, and if the work is more arduous, at least he is his own boss and very much at home in the open air. Elena is careful, however, to maintain her connections with various charitable organizations. Like her husband, she is haunted by the specter of ruin and keeps a secret reserve of cash hidden somewhere in the house. When one of her sons was arrested for minor delinquency, these funds paid for the legal fees which were necessary if he were to avoid imprisonment. If she becomes pregnant again, the money will finance an abortion. If Stefano's moving jobs slacken, or if he falls ill, it will enable her to feed her family. But a few hundred dollars hidden in a vase provides meager insurance for the ongoing lives of eight people. For Stefano and Elena, the ordinary vicissitudes of family history are major economic shakedowns which can mean reduction to a precarious day-to-day, hand-to-mouth existence. When it came time for me to say farewell to them, the Signora thought to warn me, lest I return one day and expect to find them as always: "You'll come knocking in the morning, Tom, and you'll be wondering why I greet you as always and chat with you as always, and never offer you a caffè. You won't realize that *il caffè non ce n'è* [there isn't any]."

Survival for the poor involves continuous effort but discontinuous success. Even if you try hard in the present, you can expect to be in serious need of basic commodities at some point in the future. It is not true that the poor are not cognizant of the future. They refuse to trust it, regard it as an enemy, and adjust their behavior and philosophy of life accordingly. The sporadic and unpredictable nature of economic endeavor among the underclasses of Naples is the most salient fact of their existence. One is liable and likely to be reduced at any time. For most people, the day of reckoning has already come. It will come again, and one's account of oneself and of one's fellows is always rendered in the harsh light of yesterday or tomorrow. Everyone knew everyone else at Fontana del Re. They knew each other as they knew themselves, and therefore they kept their locks in good repair.

The Picaresque Tradition

In Naples, individuals are too often forced to regard the social order as an exclusive organization. They find themselves, a great multitude, outside the gates of those structures where work and security and even minimal dignity are united in employment. It is here, in the thorny backyard of society, that the picaresque tradition takes root and thrives, like a tough weed. At an early age, the individual is thrown back upon his own capacity to master from

112

his masters the arts of deception and trickery whereby he can take his due and more.

Peppino
The first time I met him at Fontana del Re, Peppino called me Joe and took me aside and talked enthusiastically about America. After about three minutes of animated monologue, he asked me the time, but when I looked at my wrist my watch was gone. Peppino dangled the watch in front of my face to tease me with his triumph and my naiveté. As I was leaving, about a half hour later, he asked me if I didn't want my wallet back as well.

To my great annoyance, Peppino repeated these tricks whenever I encountered him. He was a nervous fellow, with slick black hair and keen relentless eyes. He rarely conversed with people, preferring to joke. Peppino worked in an auto body repair shop during the day. At night, he hung around the port to befriend tourists and American sailors. His pride as a man derived from what he did with sleight of hand.

Eduardo
Eduardo was a tall, lithe man in his early twenties, with fine angular features and a soft confused expression. He did not look like a thief, although he never hesitated to call himself one and was proud to have been interviewed by student-researchers from the university. The people of Fontana del Re had nicknamed him *il Saggio,* the wise man, as he was ready with advice at all times. Since I was obviously more in need of advice than anyone he had ever met, it was to be expected that Eduardo and I should become good friends.

Eduardo did not have a regular trade. He had worked at various odd jobs and had hated them all. He became a full-time thief in his late teens, but his specialty, house burglary, put severe demands on his nervous system and he suffered from an ulcer. His major failing as a burglar was a taste for elegant clothing. If Eduardo came across a cache of fine underwear in a drawer, he would devote as much time to collecting this finery as to the television or the stereo. Naturally, this was exasperating to his co-workers. Eduardo survived long months of inactivity by living with his mother, who sold contraband cigarettes and gave him a small allowance. He had spent six months in Germany, three months working and three months in the hospital, nursing his inflamed stomach and collecting sick pay. Finding the Germans a cold, distant people, he came home.

In February of 1975, Eduardo grew tired of his poverty and inactivity and decided to put his life in order. He applied for a part-time civil post as a night watchman and, while waiting for a decision on that, took a job as a parking attendant. But that job paid so little that he went to work as a plumber's assistant at the same time. When I hired him to do some repairs, he overcharged me for the parts; and when I complained, he became indignant and chastised me for neglecting my research and for being naive about the harsh realities of Neapolitan life.

Eduardo concluded that it was impossible for him to survive by means of part-time plumbing and parking-attending. He went back to his earlier profession, robbing only places to which he could obtain easy access. A janitor's duplicate key might admit him to a storeroom filled with surgical tools or some other impractical utensil, which he would then proceed to fence or sell at prices that were ludicrously low. Or a friend having a clandestine affair with a wealthy homosexual would give him the key at a prearranged time, and there would be a bonanza of precious underwear and clothing to divide with the accomplice.

The Triumvirate of Want

For young Eduardo, peace of mind was related to a respectable presentation of self. He took me shopping with him one sunny March afternoon. We traveled through the local quarter to two small garagelike shops with no signs. Eduardo bought some fashionable jeans and some stylish boots. He hinted to me once again that he wanted the college graduation ring that I was wearing, as a present before I went away. We both agreed that it would be a fitting memorial to the friendship we had forged. I gave my ring to Eduardo that same afternoon. Two weeks later, I saw some people admiring it on another man's finger at Fontana del Re.

Ciro

When Ciro spoke Italian, he pronounced every word carefully, pausing over each sentence to ponder the correct grammar and pronunciation of the next. But when he spoke Neapolitan, he talked so fast, his words tumbling and leaping ahead of one another, that I could rarely follow him. He was a disheveled youth, with a slightly crooked jaw and a squat nose. His father was a truck driver and his mother ran a small candy store near Fontana del Re. He and his brothers were famed in the quarter as skilled and daring thieves. Ciro could have worked with his father, but he preferred the life of the rogue and the thief. One evening, over a beer, he told me why:

> "The worker is a shit, Tommaso! He sweats forty
> hours for forty thousand lire and I sweat, maybe forty
> minutes, for the same. Sure I take chances. The other
> day I grabbed this lady's bag by the station, and the
> bitch starts to holler and won't let go. I knock her
> down, and she's yellin' and won't let go. But then the
> cops are coming, and I take off. But they're on motor-
> cycles and they would have caught me for sure if a

115

passing car hadn't stopped and let me in. They were
thieves too, helping out a colleague.

"I know I'll end up in jail, but I can take care of
myself there too. As long as I go for something big, so
that when I come out, everybody respects me, I won't
mind. I'm a nice guy, Tommaso, a friend to all; and I
never trust anyone. When I fight I get *nervoso*. I've
bitten one guy's ear off already."

Ciro's life was not as romantic as he liked to picture
it. Because of the ups and downs of petty thievery and
parental patience, he often found himself deprived of bed
and board. During such times, he resorted to male prostitution. But after such transactions he felt the uneconomi-
cal necessity of running to low-priced prostitutes to neutralize the effect of the homosexual contact. As he
explained the occupational hazards of this particular side-
line, "It's okay once in a while to screw fairies for money,
Tom, but if you do it too often, one day or another,
they're liable to flip you over and screw you!"

Ciro knew who he was, if he was a thief. Like so
many of the young men I knew at Fontana del Re, he was
proud and ashamed at once of his criminal activities. In
encounters with his working peers, he stood below them
in the moral scheme of things and was defensive and apol-
ogetic. But as a thief, determined to continue as such, he
claimed membership in a kind of secret societ,' or anti-
society which could make sense of his marginality by at-
tacking the pieties of proletarian submission and by transforming the self-interest of petty crime into the collective
heroism of primitive rebellion.

But thieves and workers alike—and the boundaries
between them were often blurred—reserved ultimate
homage for the power of wealth. The dignity of money
was greater than the dignity of labor at Fontana del Re. If a

man chose to pursue the one, he often found himself compromised with respect to the other. There is a line in Brecht's masterpiece, *Mother Courage,* where the heroine states, "pride isn't for the likes of us. You eat dirt or down you go."[8] The wealthiest person at Fontana del Re was a woman who rented rooms to prostitutes, a very lucrative activity. She was respected and envied, and even hated by a few. I rarely spoke to her, as she had a hard, distant air, but one winter evening, staring out from my balcony, I saw her gazing out from hers. Backed by the light of her crystal chandelier, she surveyed the broken stones below like a haughty old queen.

The Rites of Spring in Naples

André Gide once wrote that in the winter rains, Naples is the most lugubrious city on earth.[9] The cobblestones turn wet and slippery. The litter collects and rots in the puddles. The old women retreat into the shrine-lit darkness of their bassi. Mothers and children huddle close to their stoves, while workers rise and work and return to their tables, and sleep and rise and work again. Young men take refuge in pool rooms and bars. At night, along Via Roma and the boulevards, the whores shiver and curse by their fires. Their makeup runs in the rain.

In mid-March, early one weekday morning, my friend Stefano woke me and rushed into my apartment. He came bearing a cup of thick hot chocolate and told me it was a special day, for feasting. The pale face of his little son emerged from the darkness, all mustachioed from the cocoa. It was the Day of the Fathers and the Feast of St. Joseph. All Naples would be home for this day.

The atmosphere downtown was especially light. There was a fine spring breeze and a palpable softness in the air.

117

In the main piazza, Piazza Municipio, a bustling market of birds had been set up overnight. There were birds of all kinds but mostly chicks, squirming and huddling in baskets and cages, dyed blue and pink or left to their own natural gold. Boys rushed through the crowd, hawking goldfish and puppies. Old women, clad in black, sat like stately governesses behind their arrays of gowned dolls. Makeshift stalls sold stuffed animals and toys. Others sold neckties and sunglasses, and everywhere yellow canaries and silky blue parakeets hopped and fluttered about in wooden cages, creating a chaos of chirping.

In Naples to sell is to live. Buying and selling are the processes of life and come as naturally to the poor Neapolitan as plowing and harvesting to the peasant.

Two systems of exchange organize the buying and selling of goods in Naples. The shops along the main boulevards and avenues serve the middle and upper classes of the city. But the lower-class districts have an economy of their own, comprised of innumerable vendors selling an innumerable range of products amidst all the noise and color and fanfare of an oriental bazaar. This *economia del quartiere* or slum economy, as it has been called, is the Neapolitan little man's defense against inflation and deprivation.

Almost everyone smokes in the poor quarters of Naples. Tobacco is seen as one of life's few blameless joys. After the Sunday dinner, Signora Elena would sit back in her chair with Robertino nestled in her lap. She would take her own cigarette and place it between the boy's lips, and he would puff away as fast as he could.

Three women sold cigarettes at Fontana del Re to the people who lived there. The cigarettes were contraband and cheaper than those sold at the licensed tobacco shops. No one bought their cigarettes from the tobacco shops at Fontana del Re. Unlike vending machines or shopkeepers, the old woman whom you've known all your life is likely to let you have a few packs on credit if you're short of cash for the moment.

The police permit the continued operation of the system. It is not uncommon to see a police car stop at a stand and receive gratis a carton or a pack of cigarettes. There are periodic crackdowns; these are not directed against the large-scale *grossistas* who purchase in bulk, but against the street-vendors, who pay the fine or go to jail.

The trade in contraband merchandise in Naples is not limited to cigarettes. Stefano and Elena bought meat once a week from a wholesale meat outlet. The meat, they told me, was contraband. The radios and television sets of the people of Fontana del Re were purchased from the stalls of a certain district where the finest and most sophisticated kinds of stereo equipment were sold at discount rates. Of course, no one writes receipts in that part of town and there is, for the unwary, the risk of the *bidone;* in this trick the unwitting customer receives, instead of his television set, a nicely packaged box filled with stones and straw.

Almost anything could be purchased for less money inside the quarter. The pastries that occasionally appeared on Stefano's table came from a small bakeshop nearby which didn't bother to put up a sign. A bottle of brandy sold for five hundred lire less at a bar inside the quarter than at an establishment serving the general, anonymous public. Of course, the password into this lower system of prices is a native mastery of the Neapolitan dialect. Even inside the quarters two price systems prevailed, *prezzi Napoletani* and *prezzi Americani,* and Romans and Florentines, as well as hapless Americans, were subject to the latter system.

The thieves' markets of Naples are not organized to serve the interests of the poor. But they provide at least part of a livelihood to many people who might otherwise be idle and hungry. They provide some relief from the ravages of inflation to the hundreds of thousands of poor Neapolitans who choose to buy contraband. Moreover, by patronizing their own small vendors, the poor people of Naples do battle with taxes and inflation and, as other writers have pointed out, they ensure that their own limited supply of money passes through the hands of as many poor men as possible before it eventually and inevitably reaches the hand of a rich man.

Rents were usually lower in the poor quarters, but the apartments were small and the buildings were deteriorating. At Fontana del Re one building had already collapsed, and other structures had been condemned. Still others had been condemned and then "de-condemned." I lived in one of these "declassified" edifices. My apartment was notorious in the neighborhood for its dampness. I wondered how a child might ever thrive in such a place. The walls were thick. The fresh paint which covered them soon peeled away to reveal the gray-green beneath in strange chameleon patterns.

The people of Fontana del Re never forgot to turn their lights out and if ever I forgot to turn out mine, they reminded me in admonishing tones. They didn't have toilet seats, and for tissue they made use of other people's discarded newspapers. They wore their shoes, literally, to the ground, and they saved their buttons and zippers. When a housewife had to boil two pots of water at the same time, she rarely lit two burners, but placed one pot on top of the other, to utilize the steam and save gas. Nonperishable items like coffee and beans were often purchased in bulk, whereas perishables were purchased as they were consumed, to avoid wastage.

One night in September, I remember the dark lanes of the old quarters were lighted by fires set beneath black iron cauldrons, attended by crews of women and children. At first I suspected some obscure pagan rite of the equinox, but the tomato crop was in and the housewives were putting up their winter's supply of sauce. The poor of Naples were not by nature a frugal people with a spartan standard of living. They economized where they could so as to spend where they wanted to, and they enjoyed a period of rising fortunes with the same fierce energy with which they resisted and endured a descent into misery.

The slum economy of Naples is more than a catalogue of ingenious productive strategies and defense mechanisms against inflation. It is an expression of the poor Neapolitan's will to survive against great odds. Faced with the choice between morality and survival, the Neapolitan always chooses survival. He does not always attain survival heroically, just as he does not always suffer tragically. But ultimately he is a humanist, convinced that life is worth the effort and trouble of living, even if one is unfortunate enough to have been born a scavenger, relegated to society's lower depths.

chapter eight

Reactions to a Disordered World

Because we call you "brothers" there's no need
To be angry, although we were put to death
By justice: anyway, you understand
Not everyone is born with good sense . . .

François Villon, epitaph
"Ballade des Pendus"

THE GREAT ANARCHIST, Mikhail Bakunin, thought that poor folk like those of Naples, "being almost totally virgin to all bourgeois civilization," would lead the world to true socialism.[1] But the poor are not, alas, "virgin" to bourgeois civilization. They deal in its currency and accept its terms as servants or tricksters. In other words, they are seriously compromised and hardly in a position to fashion the organizational weaponry which is a first prerequisite for any socialism.

The Neapolitan underclasses might impede the advance of a proletarian revolution. They are quick enough to riot, but they are not a people for organized rallies and marches, unless these be corrupted with a carnival air. Their bazaars abound with small-time capitalists, and buying and selling are passion and joy with them. A humanistic socialism might tap these entrepreneurial energies, in a dynamic, mixed economic program. Indeed, if ever we could have a new order, on the poet's scheme, "without divisions of desire and terror,"[2] shouldn't ample space be provided for gypsies . . . and Neapolitans.?

123

Traditional Marxism is ambivalent toward the subproletarian poor. Among them, we can certainly locate those objects of "injustice in general" upon whom the young Marx centered his hopes for human redemption.[3] But since no capitalist-managerial class has ever organized them into worker's regiments, they are (as Marx himself realized) unlikely recruits for a protracted class warfare. Their unity is not the unity of common productive relations—the fraternity of the shop—but rather the less cohesive unity of common deprivation. The coordination of behavior and ideology which is ordinarily expected from members of the same class is present only erratically among them. They envy the wealth as they resent the power of others, but only rarely do they question the legitimacy of power and wealth.

Nikolai Bukharin, in his attempt to carry forward the Marxian analysis of class, denied class status to the lumpenproletarians and characterized them as an undisciplined and shiftless mass "whose actions are based only on foolish caprices." Whereas the ideology of the proletariat tended toward revolutionary communism, among the lumpenproletariat there was only "a vacillating and hysterical anarchism."[4] In the classic Marxian view of class conditions, then, the poor of Naples have never been and will never be historically significant. They are the underproletarians, part of that vast, inchoate crowd who only add to the noise of history and never succeed in changing its course.

How much of the history of people in cities is the anonymous progression of the lives of these wretched multitudes? What did they ask of life, these innumerable men and women, fallen from the oblivion of their lives into the deeper oblivion of death, and what did they receive? We can know very little of their aspirations, and we are familiar with only the barest details of how they lived.

Consider the ancient Roman majority as described by the historian Ludwig Friedlander:

Their dark rooms, two hundred steps up, were not as high as a man's stature. Their hearth was cold. A jug with a broken handle, a mat, a heap of straw, an empty bedstead was their furniture; a short toga by day and night their only protection against the cold; vinegar wine and black bread their food . . . [or if they suffered the common lot of eviction] their refuge in the cold rain of December might be an open archway; their dog their sole friend, and their food dog's bread . . . their wealth a staff, a blanket, or a mat and a knapsack; their salvation, solitary death. [5]

This is the brutal reality of the historical type with which we are dealing. Is the urban scene outlined by Fernand Braudel for seventeenth-century Spain so different? He identifies the squalid mass of underemployed workers and vagrants as "a structural feature of Mediterranean life since at least the twelfth century."

He writes:

In Spain the survival of ancient inherited wealth and marked demographic decline contributed in the seventeenth century to produce a strange social category, a proletariat comparable to the plebians of ancient Rome. Genuinely poor, rascals from the town whom the picaresque novel has made famous, false or authentic beggars, all this gente de hampa, *these* hampones, *tramps, had done with work maybe, but work and employment had done with them first.* [6]

Or consider the following statement by another historian, R. M. Johnston, concerning the condition of the Neapolitan *plebs* in 1800, revealing even in its probable exaggerations:

Many of them had neither family nor name; one out of three answered to that of Sposeto. *The word derived from the* esposti or *foundlings who were numerous. . . . The food of the* lazzaroni *was chiefly bread, macaroni, and fish; their usual habitations by night were baskets made of osiers. . . . Their numbers were formidable, perhaps 150,000 before 1799.*[7]

If the Risorgimento ushered the Italian peninsula into the modern arena of national development, it apparently did little to ameliorate the condition of the city poor. Giustino Fortunato, a political journalist writing in 1878, describes a seething human mass, crowded into exorbitantly priced, warehouselike tenements, infected by tuberculosis and scrofula. He focuses on one corner of central Naples, approximately 10,000 square meters in area:

It was a beehive of 8,000 inhabitants, an agglomeration of blackened structures, passageways, tiny courtyards and alleys, and tenements like ant-colonies. Each room housed a family of seven or eight persons. These rooms were without air and light and potable water as well, since the wells, situated beside the toilets, yielded only the nauseating muddy brine of the underground, worsened by proximity to the sea. . . . The majority of these tenements were owned by upright citizens, and it is curious indeed that the greater part should belong to charitable foundations. . . . The poorest newshawkers, the poorest laborers in the arsenal, and the humblest workers in the tobacco factory, as well as the most skillful smugglers, were gathered together in a kind of confusion, on this ignored, forsaken island.[8]

This is the grim reality that lies beneath the luminous surface of urbanism in the Mediterranean. If the poor could not find solidarity in their relations of production, they achieved it in misery and in the hatred that misery breeds.

But hatred is a poor organizer, and the lessons of hunger rarely expand a man's horizons. As Gramsci so well

126

understood, such hatred does not indicate an active and aware class consciousness, but is merely "the first glimmer of such consciousness . . . the basic, negative, polemical attitude." Gramsci continues: "Not only does the people have no precise consciousness of its own historical identity, it is not even conscious of the historical identity or exact limits of its adversary."[9]

As Eric Hobsbawm and George Rudé have documented them, the rebellions of such folk, whether of rural masses or city mobs, are typically phantasmagorias of savagery and hope. The people rise on a crest of near-suicidal insurrectionary zeal, and founder as quickly on their own narrow view of the enemy and their own short list of goals. The rich are slaughtered in the name of the king. The bakers are threatened. The price of bread is lowered, and the people return to their homes. The familiar rhythms of a social system founded on poverty reassert themselves inexorably. This is the political tragedy of the lumpenproletariat.[10]

The Neapolitan masses confirm the continuing validity of these generalizations. Their political energy is the energy of blind rage. As such it is easily burned out although it may serve the special interests of one elite faction against another, as in 1799, when the plebs sided with the gentry and massacred their liberal Jacobin rulers. It erupts sporadically in myriad small incidents of protest. On the Sunday afternoon of December 23, 1973, for example, angry crowds protested food shortages and a mass transit strike by beating up bus-drivers and blockading streets, creating a climate of rebellion throughout the city.[11]

The fear of hunger remains the primary sentiment that can shatter the customary political torpor of the poor quarters. In 1585 and in 1647 against the excesses of Spanish taxation, and in 1943 against the Germans and the hunger which they aggravated, the poor of Naples rose up in

127

full-scale insurrections, in hopes of improving their own desperate condition. In the decades of crisis that will close our century, I think only this same fear of hunger will waken the people from the hypnosis induced by soccer and the media, and motivate them to unite, if only briefly, against those with power. When Stefano talked of revolution, he always cited the price of food:

> "We have to buy pasta, oil, beans, bread, milk, some meat, vegetables and wine. It's all going up, up, up! It costs us 10,000 lire a day just to eat. I work only to eat and feed my family. Nothing more. There will be a revolution in Italy, Tommaso. There has to be!"

Like his neighbors at Fontana del Re, however, Stefano perceived social phenomena in personalistic, even sentimental terms. Prices rose because other people were greedy and heartless. Conditions for the poor would improve if generous rich people, as opposed to stingy ones, were in control.

The poor of Naples reacted to the events of a disordered world in a chaotic and folkloristic manner. "Italy is a poor country," they would tell me, "because the Americans stole the atom bomb away from us." This was an article of faith at Fontana del Re, and the name of Fermi had filtered down to to them as the betrayed messiah of their latent cargo cult. Once when I was planning a trip to London (which never materialized), a number of my friends told me that they had relatives nearby, in a place called Brook-a-leen. London and New York, Dusseldorf and Amsterdam, all formed part of the same foreign megalopolis to them. The world north of Rome seemed to merge in their minds into a single metropole, inscrutably powerful and wealthy but hopelessly barbaric in a cultural sense.

128

Perhaps because they had formed no coherent view of contemporary society and were inconsistent in their attitude toward the upper class, envying them and hating them but admiring them and emulating them at the same time, the people of Fontana del Re vacillated in their political allegiances and sometimes professed multiple allegiances at once. "As a worker," Stefano told me, "I can sympathize with the Communists, but I like the Fascist laws, their way of running the country." Apparently he was unaware of the Stalinist synthesis. Elena claimed that she was a Communist, which to her meant "anti-Fascist," since her father had been beaten by the Fascist police during the war. When a group of radical students demonstrated for worker's rights in the vicinity of Fontana del Re, she dismissed them, irrespective of their revolutionary ideology, as "people who have always had their heads good and close to the trough." Other people at Fontana del Re joked about their Communist sympathies. It was better to be Communist, they advised me, because that way one would be captured by the Americans in the next war. Abstract notions of social justice played a minor role in the political life of the slum.

At Fontana del Re, when people moved leftward, they usually did so to affirm themselves as free and fierce-willed individuals and not out of a sense of solidarity with other workers. My friend Gino worked in a dental laboratory preparing false teeth. "I am a Communist," he confided, "because now, if an apple falls from the desk of my *padrone*, he can look at me, and command, 'Pick it up!' " My friend had decided that communism meant liberation from all forms of authoritarian control. One of the most dedicated Communists I knew in the poor quarters was Michele, the somber dressmaker. He was proud to display volumes of Marx and Marcuse on his bookshelf, but he lived as he worked, in a world apart, and had little commitment to the practical requirements of worker organization.

The rightist sentiments of the people I knew were invariably associated with an identification with the symbolism of force and the personal qualities of the leader. Mussolini was often praised in the same enthusiastic tones reserved for John Kennedy and Pope John XXIII. A generically similar, perhaps less religious, admiration was expressed for the former boss-mayor of Naples, Achille Lauro, and his son. When I protested that the Lauro administration had been shamelessly corrupt, my friends replied indignantly, "But he gave bread to the people," referring to the free packets of macaroni which poor families used to receive during the Lauro electoral campaigns of the fifties. In a sense, Lauro was the last Bourbon. His philosophy of government resembled that of the Bourbon King Ferdinand, whose formula for city administration was simple enough—"*Festa, Forca e Farina*" (bread, feasts, and the scaffold). Even as recently as 1974–1975, on major feastdays a number of families at Fontana del Re received baskets of food from the neo-Fascist party, the *Destra Nazionale*. These baskets, I was told, were really from the son of Lauro, the current *padre di Napoli*. As Eduardo explained:

> "Lauro cleaned up the garbage at Fontana del Re. He is our benefactor, and what's more, his son is godfather to the owner of the bar around the corner. He gave millions for our local feasts. The Communists have no money. They are poor; miserable like us."

In general, however, people were not interested in political topics at Fontana del Re. In his analysis of the Neapolitan political system, Percy Allum presents ample documentation for what he terms "a profound sense of estrangement from the legal polity." Apathy toward the state, and ignorance of political events, as well as a not wholly inaccurate view of the government as a vertical network along which favors are passed sum up the political world-view of the Neapolitan underclass. The terse comment of a twenty-eight-year-old butcher's assistant, quoted by Allum, sums it up even better: "I no longer vote for anyone and the next time I shall get myself paid for my vote and go and pee in the polling booth." [12]

More than any other "political" institution of Italian society, the people of Fontana del Re were familiar with the prison. Everyone knew the basic rules and regulations of the prison, and many of the local young men assumed that they would spend a part of their lives in jail. In fact, it was impossible to obtain genealogies from the people at Fontana del Re because of anger and embarrassment at revealing the names of relatives who are in prison. In the local scale of values, if a man were sent to prison for a petty crime, he became an object of ridicule and contempt. But if he were sentenced for a more serious offense, especially a shooting, he was heroized by the local youths as a paragon of sorts, a *guappo,* deserving of admiration and respect. It did not matter whether the guappo was an arrogant bully at heart. By a series of moral reversals recalling Genet, the readiness for lethal violence (because of the Promethean defiance of legitimate authority which it implied) qualified a man for temporary sainthood.

Representatives of bureaucratic power, from tax assessors to policemen, were suspect and disliked at Fontana del Re. I was told that when the police pursued a fleeing thief into the quarter, they did so at the risk of being pelted with garbage and excrement. I cannot vouch for the truth of this assertion, but the frequency of the assertion itself illuminates the attitude. One never called the police

131

in an emergency at Fontana del Re. People who were suspected of contemplating such a move were known locally as "the spies."

In the local urban social structure, the poor viewed themselves in diminutive terms, as "the little people," or *popolino*. *I grandi signori* was the phrase they applied to all those who were elsewhere in the urban social system. A bank teller, a grocery store owner, and a millionaire were not so very far apart in their minds. I recall walking once with Stefano and Pepe through a district of middle-income housing. At one point we bought some sandwiches, and I began to eat my sandwich as I walked. Everyone else refrained from eating. I inquired why and so they told me that although it was permissible to eat in the street at Fontana del Re, here, surrounded on all sides by *i grandi signori*, it would be improper and, in fact, shameful to do so. I looked around for signs of grandi signori, but all I could see were the boorish architectural manifestations of *petit-bourgeois* consumerism.

Their class consciousness was, as Gramsci noted for the southern masses generally, negative rather than positive. Rather than conceive of themselves as part of the enduring bedrock of society, upon whose condition of servility and toil the remainder of the system implicitly depends, their self-perceptions, on an individual and a collective plane, were negative. They are those whom the larger system denies.

Perhaps this was why style was so important with the young men of Fontana del Re. For all their swagger, they yearned for acceptance by a society which had given them the snub. Style was something which they could appropriate and elaborate upon. Unlike literacy and salable skills, it was a manipulable part of social identity. Indeed, many of them risked imprisonment to dress well, not to eat.

One evening, Stefano, whose friendship was as warm

132

as it was possessive, discussed the question of our mutual equality:

> "You want to be a professor, Tommaso, and I am a laborer, and a damn good one at that! This is what makes us equal, Tom. I do my job and you do yours. Everyone here calls me *Signore,* because I'm an honest man. I tell my children to be like me. I tell them always to go with their betters, people like yourself."

Stefano's words contain, of course, a profound contradiction, just as they reveal an underlying insecurity about the foundations of his identity and the identity of his children. On a superficial level, he would convert esteem into status, but he cannot complete the exchange. On a deeper level, he is aware of the potential equality of being which he and I as men possess, but he has learned to accept a definition of self based on economic function. Because he defined being in terms of having, he experienced a kind of psychic contraction and felt himself to be a lesser man. These were common sentiments at Fontana del Re. As the unwitting representative of a higher though foreign-based class, I was assigned an emotional importance which I was not given the opportunity to earn. I was heroized or vilified. There was no middle human ground. My friends at Fontana del Re wanted me to dress well. They insisted that my trousers be pressed and my shoes polished. The situation was reminiscent of Pygmalion, except that here the professor was being taught proper manners by the cockney vendor.

In Naples, those who are born poor, die poor, and no man can expect to rise above his assigned station in life. In such a setting, the distinctions between class and caste fade. Severe psychological adjustments are required of individuals. Children must not be encouraged to expect very much from life or from themselves. The adult bestowal of hope on a child's finest potentials was forbidden at Fontana del Re. I once shouted some words of encouragement to a bright little boy, on his first day of school. Half-jokingly, I admonished him to study diligently, so that someday he might become a lawyer or a doctor. His grandmother and sister scowled at me. Others turned away. Later, his older brother explained that he would go as far as the fifth grade, and no farther. Why confuse and trouble him with futile hopes and dreams?

When Michele and Angela had a second child in March of 1975 and the infant fell ill, Angela took him to a public clinic. Although the attending physician examined the child and uttered a few words before dismissing the case as minor, he never once looked up to acknowledge in any way with his eyes the existence of the mother. A few months later, Angela took her baby to the priest for baptism. I was to be the godfather. But Michele had refused to attend, and because of this the priest refused to perform the rite. Angela pleaded and I interceded. Before consenting, he looked down at her and sneered, "Do you think we care, Signora, whether or not your child is baptized?"

The poor, especially the mothers of the poor, put up with insults such as these every day. I remember how Elena and Stefano had planned and looked forward to a one-day bus excursion to Rome with their family. When they returned, I asked them if they had enjoyed their all-too-brief vacation away from home. Elena grimaced at the question. The highlight of the day, she reported, was in the restaurant. The children wanted some fruit and Stefano, seeing that the waiter was very busy, walked over to the fruit bowl to get some. The Roman waiter rushed to his side and abruptly blocked his arm. Stefano returned to his seat, humiliated in front of his children. The waiter then carried the fruit bowl to their table and offered with all due ceremony. When he nodded to Elena, she took hold of the bowl and, wresting it from his hands, she tossed it in his face. As she attacked him, she lectured him on courtesy. The proprietors apologized and convinced her to retreat to the excursion bus. The police were not summoned. But a precious day had been ruined for Stefano and Elena and their children. It is against the backdrop of such incidents and the memory of such days that we can better understand what Richard Sennett has called "the hidden injuries of class."[13] For the individual, depending upon the strength of his or her relationship to self, the result may be akin to what James Baldwin has described as the major symptom of the racial variant of caste oppression:

A kind of blind fever, a pounding in the skull and a fire in the bowels. Once this disease is contracted one can never really be carefree again, for the fever, without an instant's warning, can recur at any moment . . . one has the choice merely of living with it consciously, or surrendering to it. As for me, this fever has recurred in me, and does, and will until the day I die.[14]

If reality is threatening to all people, it is more threatening to the poor, and they must compensate and defend themselves accordingly. If, as R. D. Laing tells us, chronic ontological insecurity gnaws at the life-force of modern man, it sucks at the bone marrow of the poor.[15] The theatrical quality of life in the poor quarters, the loud, gesticulating style and the aggressive hubris of the individual, is the Neapolitans' collective commentary on the instability of the socioeconomic and honorific settings upon which they must stage their lives.

Poverty creates a state of crisis in society as class creates a state of open and latent conflict. In crisis, men and women cannot behave out of the fullness of them-

135

selves but are constrained to operate mechanically, to attain limited objectives. People are reduced by poverty and the brand of class. They are far less than what they might be.

chapter nine

Conclusion: The Poor of Naples and the World Underclass

For Europe, for ourselves, and for humanity,
comrades, we must turn over a new leaf,
we must work out new concepts, and
try to set afoot a new man.

Frantz Fanon, The Wretched of the Earth

HUMAN HISTORY IS tragic only because it is self-aware. Men can measure and lament the distance they have traveled from each other and themselves. They can know when they are fully human and sense when they are only pre-human. Or, as Ludwig Feuerbach has suggested, they can isolate and ignore the possibilities of their humanity, preferring to displace their finest human potentials onto the idea of God.

Humanity is here conceived of as a constant, the legacy of evolution, a set of biosocial potentials for altruism and harmonious collective life. Since the emergence of stratification, man's history (his changing ways of relating to nature and to other men) has stood opposed to his humanity. The emergence of power-wielding elites at the close of the neolithic laid the basis for a new kind of anticollective society whose vastly accelerated growth was founded, not on the reconciliation of antagonisms between men, but on their origination and amplification in slavery, caste, and class.

137

Cultures organized around the exploitations and reductions of class are, in the Marxian view, bestial and not fully human.[1] The cultural differences which accumulate at different tiers of stratified systems may be summarized in descriptions of class culture. These are stratum-specific patterns of behavior, feeling, and systematized thought which may codify, justify, compensate for, and in some cases even protest the dehumanizing circumstances of life in class systems.

Classes are usually defined and recognized by their relationship to the means of production and to the surpluses which these relations of production induce. Peasantries, for example, generate agricultural surpluses which are removed from them by rent, tax, and the constraints of exchange in urban markets. Proletarians generate surpluses of commodity value which are then expropriated by means of wage-labor contracts whose legalized function is to take out more than they put in. The vast surpluses collected by the managerial elites of states go to maintain and refine the machinery of surplus extraction and to finance the sumptuary, aesthetic, and philosophical elaborations of high culture.

The conditions of peasant and proletarian existence are determined, at bottom, by the requirements and burdens of surplus production and the limitations (economic and cultural) which these requirements impose. Workers and peasants toil, in factories and in fields, and toil is the central organizing activity of their social and mental lives.

The labors of peasants are rhythmic in time and space. The seasonal and daily movements from hearth to field, the drag of draft animal and plow, the cutting of furrows, all the thousand skills associated with sowing, harvesting, winnowing, and storing combine to form a slow, pained ballet of bending, bowing, and praying to earth and to divine and secular masters.

The work of factory laborers is a stiff military drill, a regiment of arms welded to metal bars and wheels. Marx, Veblen, and Charlie Chaplin have powerfully made the point that, on the assembly line, man neither makes nor uses his tools but is continuous with tool as a minute, final attachment to the massive industrial machine.

The organization of group existence, the structure of collective sentiments, and the quality of day-to-day intellections—in other words, the style of life of any category of persons—is conditioned by their position and role in what Robert Redfield termed the technical order.[2] What Redfield called the moral order is always stretched on the rack of imperatives given by the technical.

Peasants and proletarians are included as indispensable components of stratified societies. But underproletarians, like the poor of Naples, do not readily find their place in the productive scheme, unless we view them as immobilized segments of the "industrial reserve army." Although they may specialize as artisans, street vendors, repairmen, scavengers, thugs, or pimps, they have no vital, sustaining role to play in the technical order of things. They are not exploited for a sizable surplus because they are never induced to yield one. Instead they are denied access to all surplus. They are left, as Marx pointed out, to gather up the leavings and the crumbs. They are the excluded, the outcasts, of antiquity and modernity alike.

Lumpenproletarians are the displaced persons of the world, and the broken city slums and shantytowns of the world are their camps. Fanon called these people the damned of the earth, and for all his hope that from this human rubble a new man would arise, damned they remain! The damned of Harlem and the South Bronx, the damned of Calcutta and Naples, the damned of Singapore and San Salvador and Manila; all these unskilled, unregi-

139

mented, but endlessly resourceful masses, laboring here one day and there another, idle and then not idle, starving and then not starving, alternating always between today's hope and tomorrow's despair; all these men, women, and children, with their eyes like wolves' eyes, constitute a single if ignored human type who may have far more in common with one another (beneath their apparent cultural differences), than anyone has yet imagined or attempted to verify. But in their own lives they remain hidden and unheard, unknown and difficult to know.

And the poor of Naples? In an economic sense, they live at the edge of the world. Their social behavior reflects the precariousness of their position. They call and cling to one another to keep from falling off, but just as often they push and trample one another down in their frenzy to survive. Poverty and scarcity bear down hard and provide the keynote for the pace and activity of their lives. Their *vicoli* appear anarchic and disarrayed, a sensuous rush of colors, a confusion of voices, as each individual hastily constructs, always ready to abandon, this day's or month's or year's patchwork for the getting of daily bread.

Politically, they are justly cynical. Long familiar with the parasitism and corruption of established bureaucratic power, they are hesitant to align themselves with the revolutionary programs and rising fortunes of other more powerful classes, whether liberal bourgeois or proletarian. They remain attached to the personalistic hierarchies of traditional authority. If disappointed or angered, they express their grievances in personalistic terms, seeking blood vengeance in sporadic outbursts of mob rage.

In a cultural sense, they are at once excluded and highly selective. By preference they speak and pass on to their children their own language and are content to learn some fragmentary standard Italian in a few years of pri-

140

mary school. They preserve a Catholic ritual façade but prefer their many Madonna-goddesses to Christ and maintain an active belief in myriad local house-spirits, reminiscent of a pre-Christian epoch. They take from the media only that which is relevant to their lives. But the mass entertainment of escapism, in music, television, and film, appeals to them as to all oppressed peoples, as a coca to numb the hunger pangs of the mind.

Do they have a "culture of poverty?" In many respects, they fulfill the requirements of Oscar Lewis's disconnected trait lists.[3] They are unemployed and underemployed. They suffer from chronic shortages of cash. They tend not to plan too far into the future. They do not trust banks or department stores. They are violent, gregarious, and resigned. Nuclear families are the rule, and mothers are important.

But many of these traits are derivatives of the first two—instability of employment and insufficiency of funds. The poor hesitate to plan for the future because they are hard-put to stay afloat in the present, and not because of a "present-time orientation." They have no trouble recalling the high and low points of their past. Their avoidance of banks relates to a realistic fear of inflation and a realistic mistrust of the literate officialdom. They do not patronize department stores because they prefer to cultivate their own, more personalized networks of local credit, marketing, and exchange. In direct contradiction to Lewis's formulation, the poor of Naples purchase vital supplies wisely and in bulk. They place numerous cultural controls on consumption, wasting nothing. They are habituated to delaying gratifications in terms of clothing, housing, plumbing, heating, travel, transportation, and entertainment. If in good times they allow themselves the one luxury of channeling surplus funds into good, abundant food,

141

I think it ethnocentric to label them irrational or immature, since this is how they sublimate a historically inherited and confirmed terror of hunger.

Confronted by a scarcity of opportunities, they become resigned, to preserve their sanity, and do not think to transcend their condition so long as they remain in underdeveloped Naples. Confronted by a scarcity of resources which, they note, does not apply to society as a whole, they become skilled in the arts of negative reciprocity. Their social relationships acquire a double-edged quality insofar as they recognize mutual and intense needs and the ruthless desperation which these same needs call forth. Confronted by the chaotic, crowded maze of the city (what Ortega y Gasset called "the plenitude" of urban life), they become violent, gregarious, or rowdy in accordance with the changing circumstances of crowded, changing scenes. The largest domestic group which they can regularly maintain is the nuclear family, and the only relationship therein which can regularly be relied upon is that with the mother, since the division of labor places her in a strategic nutritive, tactile, and psychological position.

Lewis's "culture of poverty" conception has some descriptive merit when applied to the poor of Naples, but it remains unsatisfactory because its trait lists magically transform contingent effects into causes. Moreover, applied to the poor of Naples, such a concept does not do justice to the fullness of their life-ways. They have a culture that is simultaneously against poverty, adapted to the stresses of poverty, and mangled by poverty. But they have a culture which is also fashioned out of a great Mediterranean tradition, in the crucible of a great Mediterranean city. Their culture reflects their various and ingenious strategies for survival and their low position in a hierarchy, in other words, it is a class culture as well as a regional one. Gradually they will share in a national

142

heritage. But poverty is no keystone to their world. They would do well enough without it. Their Hellenic sense of themselves as individuals demanding a place and a hearing, their spontaneity, the joy they take in feasting, their impulsive and generous sociality, the grace of their hospitality, the distinctive cadences of their speech, and their songs, with their doleful, haunting notes and their ribald, ironic, or comic appreciations—these things are no more bonded to poverty than are the vines and the flowers that grow out from the ancient stones of their houses. All the more reason then to lament the tragedy of their past and present condition.

The Neapolitan urban poor are fashion-wise, street-wise, and urbane. They are not provincial. They live close to the gates of power in the wards of a great city, but unlike proletarians they are not integrated into the political and ideological currents of mass culture. They inhabit a world connected and apart from the main, a dense and crowded urban world, submerged; a crude, loud, pushy world where the moral order is exposed as a fraud which conceals the historical ascendancy of cunning and force.

Cunning and force, the *materia prima* of life in the poor quarters.

Cunning is more than a habit of mind among the Neapolitan poor. It is a vital sign, a life-function. One eats and sleeps and breathes and is cunning to stay alive. Since the Neapolitan is denied the opportunity to earn a living in the usual fashion, by creating a surplus for expropriation, and since he is denied access to surpluses created by others, he learns to think like a thief. Although few Neapolitans actually rob for a living, the thief or *picaro* is a social prototype and gives the cue for the stereotype by which other Italians seek to dismiss him. Cunning, or *la furbizia*, is a stance which is maintained toward society as a whole, not only toward members of other classes but equally toward

143

one's neighbors, kinsmen, and friends. Other social impulses to cooperation, protection, friendship, and love must compromise and coexist or be defeated by cunning.

Force, as Simone Weil uses the term, is the central factor in history, is the capacity to turn another person into an object, to annihilate him.[4] This force is the life-beat of all slums. One does not have to attend the raucous, packed, plebian movie-houses of Naples, showing week after week the same brand of Kung-fu or shoot-'em-up Western, or participate in their endless contests of physical strength to realize that poor people respect and even worship force. Force, after all, has made them what they are and force keeps them where they are. Force has invaded their neighborhoods. Historically and daily it has created havoc in their piazzas and streets. It knocks hard on the doors of their homes. Force sits at the tables of families, to be honored and ingested by all, like communion.

At Fontana del Re in a corner strewn now with rubble, beneath the bruised, shattered visage of a lion, the eroded figure of a sculpted stone sea shell recedes into a wall.

"This was our fountain," they told me. "Oh you should have seen it, Tommaso. The water played night and day. In summer, the children scampered about in it. At night, falling asleep, you heard it, and it was like music." The young men told me it was they who had destroyed it. As children, many years before, with iron rods, they had gone every day to hammer and smash it, until they were satisfied and there was nothing left to break.

Thereafter, whenever I passed that ruined corner, I tried to imagine what the fountain had once been like, and thought and wondered and sorrowed, the more as I understood how it came to be broken.

144

Return to Naples

I HAVE RETURNED to Naples many times. Each return was a time of hope and fear. Each was a search for atonement, reunion, and forgiveness. In Naples, I never had to look for lost friends. I was soon enough recognized, waved to, and shouted at from across crowded piazzas—rushed, embraced, questioned, and finally scolded for having stayed away for so long.

It was thus, on a balmy afternoon in September of 1983 that Giuseppe, or rather, Pepe, found me on Via Roma as I stared vacantly into a shop window. Giuseppe was the son of Stefano and Elena, and he knew that I was in town, since I had already visited his parents twice, without ever finding him at home. I remembered his soft clear eyes, forlorn and wondering, and his sandy, cornsilken hair. I remembered how, in the midst of violent family quarrels, hidden in the folds of the tablecloth, he would tug ever so gently at my trousers. I would lift him into my lap and he would drift into a deep sleep as I chatted with his father. As we exclaimed over the transformations wrought in both our appearances by the passage of eight years, I recalled the circumstances of our last meeting.

Sometime in early May of 1975, shortly before my departure from Naples, I realized that I had not seen Pepe for about two weeks. I had already strained my relationship with Stefano and Elena—having intervened during a particularly brutal beating of their outcaste son, Pasquale, that followed upon his release from the hospital. I hesitated to inquire too insistently after the whereabouts of another child. I was, after all, their "adopted" son and owed my acceptance and integration into the life of the neighborhood in large measure to their generosity and warmth. But knowing that I would soon depart, I purchased a gift for my "little brother" and, after the customary Sunday meal, asked Stefano and Elena where I might find him and whether anything was wrong. "Not at all! Pepe is fine. In fact, this afternoon we are going to visit him. Come with us! Come Tommaso!" So I accompanied them on a long drive down the winding road to Pompei through the overbuilt and overpopulated towns that are crammed into the narrow stretch of plain that separates Vesuvius from the sea. Stefano turned off on a side road, wreathed on all sides by vineyards and lemon trees, their shiny young leaves a rich emerald green under a cool wash of bright yellow sunlight.

We pulled into the parking lot of a boarding school. Stefano led us into a large gymnasium where at least fifty boys were milling about or playing soccer. Immediately, I recognized the faces of children that I had last seen on the alleyways and steps of Fontana del Re and realized only then that I had not noted their absence in my journal. Stefano had located Pepe in the crowd and he came forward to meet us. He did not smile. Elena, who had left my gift of some T-shirts at home, began to unwrap a parcel of food, helpings from the courses served earlier at home. Pepe ate passively. I was troubled. Why was he here? What had he done? I knelt down beside him and asked him if he was alright but he stared so blankly that I thought, "He does not even know who I am." When I reached for his hand, he turned away, annoyed. His parents were casual and abrupt. Within twenty minutes we were driving back home. I later learned from Stefano that the State subsidized the costs of boarding the child and even paid a modest monthly stipend to the parents. The experience would be good for the boy. He would learn how to speak Italian and ply a trade.

The young man who recognized me on Via Roma was tall, lanky, and broad-shouldered, stylishly if simply dressed, with chiseled, angular features and well-trimmed light brown hair. He was eighteen years old now. He had a job as a mechanic and a winning way with young ladies. As we walked toward the garret near Piazza Dante that I had rented for the year, Pepe talked about his father and the bad times of the past winter, when moving jobs had fallen off and, to make matters worse, someone had lifted 150,000 lire ($100) from Stefano's wallet. Pepe was saving up to make a present of the stolen money for his parents.

My "apartment" had once been the dining room of a great and noble house, dating from the eighteenth century. The gold brocaded wallpaper still clung in tatters to the walls and a chandelier encrusted with grease and dust hung from the center of a high ceiling. Termites and ants were taking a steadily mounting toll on the elaborate carved paneling that gave off a faint but distinct odor of varnish and woodrot, an odor that bothered me not less but more, as the months of my return visit to Naples passed by. But Pepe was clearly impressed by the elegant, if decaying, appointments. He accepted my offer of some brandy and I began to ask about his brothers, about Ciro who was in prison and Pasquale who had "fled" to Germany. He began to tell me about his visit with Pasquale. Pasquale worked in a pizza parlor in Düsseldorf and had made a good adjustment to German life. Unlike his brother, Pepe could neither master the language nor endure the contempt that he detected in the attitude of the Germans toward their immigrant guest workers. Nevertheless, he stayed long enough "to pull a yellow number" and spent a few weeks in a German hospital recovering from a severe bout of gonorrhea. Pepe asked if he could have more brandy. Within a few minutes, he had fallen asleep on the mattress that I had set up on the floor in lieu of a bed. When he awoke an hour later, he didn't seem to know where he was. When he got his bearings, he asked me for some aspirin and a loan of five thousand lire and promised to come visit me again soon.

Pepe came by several times in the fall of 1983. He would find me at home in the late afternoon and share a drink with me before taking his customary nap. Before he left, he asked for small cash loans that we both knew he would never repay. Once, he brought a young woman with him, a lovely, if scruffy-looking blonde runaway from the north, who had been, in some way, "abused" by her father and who was now homeless. Could she use the bathtub that I shared in the hall to bathe and to wash her clothes? I encountered this girl a few weeks later, late one night under a streetlight near the port. Her crimson lipstick was thick and waxy as a child's crayon, under the harsh neon glare.

On the morning of November 10, Pepe showed up by himself. I asked him if he needed money. He did not. He had come to confess. Confess what? He couldn't say. So I invited him to walk with me down Via Roma toward the Galleria, where we could have a coffee in one of the sidewalk cafès. The crowds on the sidewalk were robotic, hard and rushing, as they tend to be in Naples and in New York. I was glad for the wintery sunshine and the slight invigorating chill that made one almost welcome the challenge of fighting one's way upstream. Pepe squinted and dug his hands deeper into his jacket pockets. His skin was pale and poor-looking. I assumed that the girl was in some sort of trouble. He stopped, immobile and mute in the middle of the sidewalk. "Why was I ever born, Tommaso?" How should I respond? How could I think of a reply that wouldn't

148

sound trite or sermonic? But before I could answer him, he blurted, "I'm a drug addict, Tommaso. I'm a junkie!"

The street noise faded away as he told me the story of how and when it had all happened. It began sometime after the earthquake of 1980, when he was sixteen, and no longer at the *Istituto*. It grew very serious, very quickly, involving the consumption by injection of 1.5 grams of heroin per day, as well as Valium and other "downers" in excessive doses. He then described the effect of the drugs. It was "bella," he said, "to have your headphones on, the music blasting, the people small and miniaturized, the colors of stoplights and signs melting and then bursting all around you in vivid explosions, Indeed, it was as if you could see all of Naples, with all of its people and events and private lives and loves hidden from the ordinary view. It was as though you could see the whole city, reeling and swirling and rocking before your very eyes." His face shone with a mystic's vision of ecstacy. But then he spoke of how horrible it was to be so stupefied, so numbed to all feeling. "I felt nothing, Tommaso. Not a thing. Just nothing, nothing, nothing!" He told me of his devotion to a fourteen-year-old girl with whom he had first shared his habit and his drugs. One night, desperate and shaking, she implored him to go out and hustle for a fix. When he returned with the goods, she was stone-cold dead, having o.d.'d on her own hidden stash.

Pepe was surprised and pleased by my non-judgmental stance of calm clinical detachment. He described a wide range of substances and discussed, with an air of medical authority, their recommended (psychotropic) dosages and their optimal and adverse effects. It was clear that he knew a great deal about and admired the efficiency of the pharmaceutical technology presently available for the successful transport, anesthesia, and excision of human souls.

149

"How much does all this cost?"

"I need at least 150,000 lire a day to shoot up the way I like. I snatch purses. I'll let a faggot get close and then kick the shit out of him to get his wallet. Or I'll go up to where all the engaged couples park at night, and pull a gun on 'em while they're goin' at it. I don't like to do it. I always explain that I'm a junkie and that I have to have the money. I know my blood is dirty. I overdosed three times already this year. The last time they hooked me up to a machine that cleaned all my blood and I stayed off the stuff for six weeks. Now I'm still off, but I don't think I can stay away. I punched my boss in the face the other day because he raised his voice at me. You see, Tommaso, if I don't go back on, I'll crack up. I'll explode. But if I do go back on . . . I got to get back into a hospital. But they threw me out last time I went. I got to get my blood flushed clean again. There's this priest in Sanità who my brother Gennaro knows who gets these devils out of your blood."

"You mean an exorcist?" He nodded. Then he pulled up the sleeves of his jacket and showed me the scars of countless tiny needle punctures on his arms. Even as I winced, I had the distinct impression that he wanted me to react with revulsion, as though his own sense of self would somehow acquire more substance if I would only classify him as an official victim.

I tried to assure Pepe that, in achieving awareness of the destructive aspects of his addiction, he was giving evidence of an inner strength. As we walked, I reminded him of his many years at the Institute and told him of our last encounter and of how, even then, he had seemed numbed to all feeling and how such reactions were attempts on the part of the wounded to protect and heal the wound. When he inquired as to why, if his parents really loved him, they sent him away, I was at a loss for words. I told him that their love for him was real enough but that it had been

150

"buried" or, rather, "entombed." He liked the metaphor. In fact, he seemed relieved to have it and, in later conversations, would speak of the "sepulchral" love of his mother and father. He paused again, head down, in the middle of the sidewalk. He thought hard and then he asked me, "But Tommaso, why are the fathers so cruel?" I reminded him of the terrible pressures that his parents had endured, trying to raise six children in relative poverty, and then I told him a lie. I told him that when he was away and I had passed through Naples on brief summer visits, they had always spoken to me of him. His face lit up in a flash of joy, recalling that earlier expression of bliss that he had when describing the effects induced by the drugs. I bought him a coffee and asked him if he would like a yogurt. He'd never heard of yogurt and so I tried to explain what it was. He sampled a "tutti frutti" yogurt, the sweetest I could think of, and then added two heaping tablespoons of sugar. Thus corrected, he relished it and we spoke of its cleansing effects on the stomach and the blood.

"Perhaps, Pepe, you need to get in touch with that other mother."

"What mother?"

"You know, the mother who weeps now for all the lost boys of Naples." Pepe looked at me, distressed and angry. He tore open his shirt to reveal his chest, to show me the empty place where her medallion should have been.

"That's how much she means to me now, Tommaso." We walked along in silence. He was troubled. I knew he was pondering my question. Then he asked when we might meet again. He told me that he had come looking for me many times but that the concierge had sent him away. I told him to make sure to always leave a message indicating where and when I could find him, and embraced him, pressing a few bucks into his palm. To my surprise, he tried to give the money back but I insisted. So he laughed and told me he was off for a second taste of the strange exotic yogurt. From the severe ashen marble steps of the great headquarters of the Banco di Napoli, I watched him as he darted to and fro among the weaving lines of the noonday traffic until he eventually disappeared.

All afternoon and into that night, I thought about the fate of Pepe and recalled the question put to me by another boy, many years before. "Is there justice anywhere, Tommaso? Is there justice in America?" Young Guido was long dead, as no doubt was the songbird whose freedom he had once risked jail for. He had been stabbed in an argument, and had been left to bleed and pant his life out, face down on the dank cobblestones of some hustler's back alley. I had been told of this many years before by my friend Carlo, who had read an account of Guido's violent end in a local tabloid. At the time, I had hidden my grief under the cloak of "critical philosophy," but now I clenched and pounded my fists against the desk in stupid, futile rage. If I could not pray, I might at least call down curses on those responsible for Guido's corruption and death and Pepe's addiction.

"Oh little brother," I thought, "your arms have been pierced by the tiny fatal arrows of the Kingdom of the Small. Let heavy stones be tied around their necks . . ."

"But Tommaso, why are the fathers so cruel?" Pepe's question resounded in my brain and later, when at last I fell asleep, it became a distant echo, growing louder, a pitiful refrain drawing me to the edge of a deep well into which a child had fallen or been dropped. Climbing down into the frightful dark pit, I reached toward the body, curled there and shivering in an icy muddied pool. A little boy seized my hand. He clung to me and shook with all a small boy's terror of the creatures of the night. But could this lonely hunter, himself benumbed and fatigued from long wandering in the fog—could he now find the strength to raise them both up and out of the frozen earth, to a warm and sun-lit place? I awoke trembling and cried out for help. Lying awake until dawn, I asked myself how many children have perished down there, their cries unheard or unheeded by passing hunters? Alone and abandoned, they expire slowly in a cold, wet spider-ridden tomb.

In the days that followed I fell ill with a high fever. But the torment of confinement in my musty little room was worse than the prospect of perishing—teeth chattering—in a rat-infested gutter. So at night I would arise like a sleepwalker and wander through the downtown area in a quest for old friends and once familiar places that I would never find again.

On one such night, the entire city seemed prostrate before the immense FERNET BRANCA sign that bathed the stately Angevin castle in obscene white light. Where the all-night Pizzicato bar and pizzeria had once stood, with its carnivalesque cast of sailors, whores, transvestites, and con-artists, now was the Savings Bank of the Holy Ghost. Nocturnal humanity was banished. Heaps of stinking trash accumulated against the useless sunken ruin of a medieval cloister, while the one banal skyscraper, the Jolly hotel, looked down on the deserted piazza, fat, squat, self-satisfied, and triumphant. A commercial mural for yet another after-dinner liqueur caught my eye. *Digerire e vivere* was its motto—"Digest and Live!"

As in the cities of the American West, the metabolism of this new Naples was increasingly petrol-based and vehicular. Its shrill clarions of vitality were the sounds of screeching tires, the nervous honking of ten thousand horns, and the primitive desperate claims of motorcycle exhaust. In the alleyways of the earthquake-scarred Quarters, the ancient music of the dialect was muffled by the unison echo of Japanese cartoons or some dubbed Amer-

153

ican oil baron or cop saga, turned up to maximum volume.

I went into a tavern, furnished and decorated in Bavarian style, that my friends from Fontana del Re had introduced me to many years before in hopes that I might assist them in their work as "tour guides" for American sailors. The fleet was not in that week and the place was desolate, except for several aging prostitutes, scattered about like dormant reptiles, ready to pounce upon and desanguinate any hapless Nebraskan farmboy who might wander in unawares. The owner, who was known to the sailors as "Tony," recognized me immediately, despite the intervening decade, and proceeded to complain wearily of the fleet's changed itinerary. As we spoke, one of the women called to me by name. Looking across the room, I noticed a portly, disheveled blonde, straight out of a painting by Hals, guzzling a glass of red wine and smiling broadly. Her mouth was stained dark purple. Two of her front teeth had either fallen or been knocked out and the gaping holes in her smile were cavernous and black. When she spoke in slurred, British-accented English, I recognized the husky tones of a voice that could not belong to the puffy, toothless hag beckoning to me so insistently. But it was Leah, who, in that other time, hovering on the threshold of this profane decline, had managed to convince me that some whores did, in fact, have "golden hearts." I embraced her mightily. She pulled away from me and laughed. Her hazel eyes danced toward the bar and she ordered me a drink. Then, wickedly, she toasted my recently acquired status of "professore." She, herself, had only recently been "graduated" from prison. Having been sent back to Denmark, she had reentered Italy illegally.

Leah had been born into an upper-class Jewish family from Copenhagen. When she was in her early twenties, she met a young Italian circus performer and fell in love with him. Leaving her parents, husband, and infant son

154

behind, she traveled across Europe with him until he, in turn, abandoned her in Milan. When I first met her in 1974, in the same tavern, Leah was approaching forty and had become a figure of some notoriety in the castrati-ruled world of the Neapolitan demimonde. Perhaps because of her striking Nordic beauty, she dared to operate independently, successfully foiling the efforts of the many pimps who tried to control her. She was an accomplished polyglot, speaking and reading fluent English, Italian, French, German and, later I learned, Hebrew. Her mastery of the Neapolitan dialect and its nuances confounded my friends, who had introduced me to her on a bet, as a crude joke, suggesting that perhaps I might succeed where they had failed.

Leah chose to live and work in Naples. It was a port city and well-adapted to her calling, but it was clear that Naples had seduced her for the same reasons that the circus had. Indeed, she had become one more rouged masquerader in its nightly theater and feast of fools. Both she and I recognized each other immediately as professional strangers, yearning, even striving, for unity with the host culture but never openly confessing our desire that it remain exotic and mysterious in the face of our harshest scrutiny. In 1974, Leah lived in a room in the heart of the Spanish Quarter, a district that was known for prostitution. She kept her private and professional lives separate, and never brought clients back to her modest book-lined lodgings. The room had a balcony that looked down on a fish market and glanced upward at a gnarled bough of wisteria that, in April, spread its pendant clusters of lavender across the pungent alleyway like a festive bridal garland. Apparently, the early morning chorus of the fishmongers didn't bother Leah in the slightest. She would get up around noon (so as to get to the bank before closing) and fling open the shutters, drinking in the hot, bright sunlight and,

155

what's more, forgiving it. I was always amazed at the way she greeted the old women seated and sewing below, calling out to them in vigorous dialect, miming their hand gestures and remonstrating with them as though she and they shared membership in a secret sorority that transcended the boundaries of culture. Then, with an insider's wit that was too rapid-fire and ribald for me to follow, she effectively dispatched, in laughter, each of the bantering vendors who winked and waved his wares at her, before ordering one of the espresso delivery boys, scurrying on the street below, to stop staring and bring her breakfast "a presto!"

Leah asked for another glass of wine but the owner, who seemed genuinely irritated by our display of mutual affection, refused her and announced that he would soon be closing. Leah stood up and lost her balance. She was struggling with her coat and muttering incomprehensibly. The other women exchanged a knowing sneer with Tony, and as I helped Leah out the door, they regarded the two of us with puzzled contempt. Drunken sailors and mercenary prostitutes gave them their formulae for order. We were after all, both, in some sense, out of place.

As I accompanied Leah home, the extent to which alcohol had ravaged her mind and body became more apparent to me. She stumbled and fell twice. But she was eager to talk and spoke, at turns, wistfully and sardonically of her past lovers, some of whom I knew, and of their various fates—noble, tragic, pathetic, but mostly ridiculous, as they thrashed about in the quicksands of mid-life. We passed through her old neighborhood, under the balcony where I would always hold her buxom, laughing image framed in memory, a hybrid cross between Carmen and Mae West. We paused. The building, along with thousands of others, had been condemned and evacuated after the earthquake of 1980. The structures nearby still bore the marks of that catastrophe—the black steel monkey bar type scaffolding that kept the old tenements from crashing inward upon one another and the oddly rustic logs that formed a sinister fretwork in every archway and stairwell. Approximately a third of the local population had been displaced to trailer camps and second-class hotels near the stadium to await the construction of large public housing projects on the periphery of the city. Gone were the little markets, hung with their beaded strings of lights and fewer were the flapping blue and white banners of afternoon laundry and sky. Nothing remained of the green vines that once softened these cracked and pitted facades. Leah's face contorted with pain. She waved her arm angrily toward a heap of rubble where the fish stalls had been.

"It is vanished, Tommaso. It will never revive. My Napoli—there was a culture here, no? Una cultura popolare? You're the anthropologist! A culture that had endured for centuries is destroyed now forever. Finito! Morto! What I loved here, what was once so alive, now is dead."

"But is it a case of murder or suicide?" I wondered aloud, recalling that the culture of the urban poor had once taken shape in the palaces of the rich and had never been impervious to the ceaseless currents of historical change.

But no matter. The world that Leah had known and celebrated was shattered. She wept softly against my shoulder. But she refused to let me walk her all the way home. The man that she was living with now was fierce and jealous. Just out of jail, he would surely beat her mercilessly if he saw her accompanied home by a younger man. "Shalom," she whispered, as she kissed me goodbye. I never saw her again.

It was during my second stay in Naples that I began to seriously question the legitimacy of my personal claim to those funds of cultural and private knowledge that had

157

provided the foundations not only of cultural anthropology as an academic discipline but of my own career as a researcher, a professor, and a writer. In 1974, as a graduate student at Columbia, I had been trained to ask probing questions of others, never to question myself as to whether I had justifiable reason or any right whatsoever to ask such questions in the first place or to publish the answers. Graduate students prepared themselves for "the field." Their status as fledgling practitioners of a scientific discipline did not exempt them from those displays of humility and obedience that are required of all ritual initiates. Indeed, unless they weathered the rigors and trials of both "fieldwork" and "write-up," they would not be admitted to the privileged ranks of the profession. But in 1984, I did not return to Naples as an idealistic student, confident (as I had been in 1974) that my research would be valued by its subjects for the same reasons that my colleagues and readers valued it. I already knew that, in writing *The Broken Fountain,* I had committed an act of betrayal, but I hoped that I would get away with it again.

My second project would follow in the footsteps of Oscar Lewis' classic *The Children of Sanchez.* After painstakingly recording the life histories of the people described in my first book, I would edit and arrange the rich and dramatic materials that I had collected and thus produce an interwoven tapestry of poor people's biographies, a document that would be both test and testament to the human capacity to convert suffering into wisdom. Certainly the people of Fontana del Re would respond with enthusiasm to the idea of such an exciting project. Stefano and Elena would be eager to help. I went looking for them on a hot muggy July afternoon. About ten days had elapsed since my arrival.

I took the long way to Fontana del Re and wandered through a labyrinth of desolate alleys, stinking of urine and uncollected heaps of smouldering, half-burned, black plastic trash bags. The truth was that I was afraid to go back to Fontana del Re. I stopped in the middle of a small piazza nearby, paralyzed with indecision, drenched in an acid sweat that seared my forehead and burned my sides. I was trembling. Had I been stricken down by the intense heat? The whitened face of an old whore, her lips parting to release and exhibit a lively flickering red tongue, leered and beckoned from the darkness of a gutted French window. Was "she" a transvestite? No matter. Her paltry life had taught her nothing except how to better endure pain. It all seemed so shabby. Why had I chosen to specialize in the phenomenology of shabbiness? An unexpected blast of hot wind engulfed me in a spiral of candywrappers and dust that would surely infect my nostrils and my eyes. What table of meanings could I possibly hope to decipher from the scarred surface of this alien southern place, this world on the wane, fallen and full of loud folk, full of so many loud blaring things, enormous radios and oversized televisions, wheezing motorbikes, squabbling, overexcited children, howling wives and mothers, the boys playing and shouting soccer in every bull-dozed, rubble-strewn lot, the men talking and arguing soccer in every bar and caffè, a whole city obsessed with soccer and given over to the adoration of its bought-and-sold player-celebrities? But worst of all, I thought, were those same scowling, spitting hags, peering out from their seemingly indestructible balconies, omniscient, wise in all the essential human things, wise in ways that mocked my booklearning and my hard-earned knowledge of anthropology.

The thought of anthropology snapped me to attention, prompting me to resume my journey, down a series of stone steps, and round a few more corners, until I stood beneath the boarded-up window of my former dwelling. The fountain was still in ruins, but a shrine to the Madonna dell'Arco had been restored and even decorated with lighted candles and fresh carnations. Did the Madonna's apparent well-being signify a revitalized neighborhood? I proceeded to the steps of the old tenement, four flights up to Stefano's apartment. Elena was on the landing outside, hanging laundry. If anything she looked younger, with frosted blonde hair and a flowered yellow housedress replacing the more familiar black of mourning. Before I could utter the word "Signora," she gasped my name, "Tommaso." I could hardly speak as she embraced me formally and took me by the arm inside, reproaching me for not having sent telegrams on Easter as well as Christmas. "Are you remarried now?" Her eyes widened in anticipation of an affirmative reply. I wavered on the ledge of a lie. I knew that all that mattered here was a "yes" or "no" answer and that "yes" was right and "no" was wrong, an unequivocal sign of failure. I withered under her stern cross-examiner's gaze.

"No."

Elena looked down and away from me, in regret more than reproach. I would have to endure the shame that she felt must attend a mature adult male's single status. Of course, I knew that she was searching for some common human ground, some way of locating my specific individuality within the framework of a shared morality, one that admitted of at least some universal convictions as to how a life should be planned and lived.

"And what of your daughter? She would be fifteen now, no? Let's see her picture? Ahhh . . . she's beautiful! Is she engaged yet? Why don't you let her stay with me for a few weeks. Well, at least, *she* will be married soon. Would you like some coffee?"

I was seated at a large glossy formica dining table. The decor had changed dramatically. Where there had once been a scratched-up mahogany china closet, now stood a large Scandinavian-style wall system, shiny black, with lots of glass compartments and chrome trim. An impressive collection of premium Scotches and gift-decantered liqueurs formed the centerpiece of the ensemble while other niches held an assortment of framed color family and wedding photographs, artificial floral pieces, "Mother's Day" ceramics, a color television, and an encyclopedia. The beaten-up brass chandelier with its dark glittering tears of chipped red glass had been replaced by a lamp that matched the wall system motif of black and chrome. Its four frosted globes of white light hung stiffly from the ceiling. The Signora returned from the kitchen with a steaming cup of espresso and sat across from me. It was strange for both of us to be alone together for so long.

"Stefano had to go to Palermo on a moving job."

"In this heat? He still works as hard as he used to?"

"Harder, Tommaso, it never gets better . . . In fact," she half-whispered, "I work now too. I take care of two well-off little old ladies up in the Vomero. I have to take the uptown bus every morning. I clean for them, make them lunch, take them out for walks."

"That's a long bus ride. It must be hard to go back and forth like that and keep two households going at once."

Elena sighed. "That's not the worst of it. You know about Ciro, no? That he's . . ." She spread the fingers of her right hand across her eyes, to make the sign for imprisonment. "That's right, you sent him that postcard a few years back, when he first went in, telling him to 'have courage,' as if he were a scared little puppy." Her laughter was gentle but nonetheless mocking.

"How is he? Is he alright?"

"Alright?" she chided, "He's the *capo* of his cellblock." She frowned. "He got fat in jail, but he's made something of himself. He's a *guappo* now, a man to be reckoned with. When he gets out, maybe he will be *capo-*

161

zona, the boss of the neighborhood. Eight years he got, because of the recent crackdown on the camorra."

"You mean, the 'maxi-inchiesta.' " Ciro had gone to work as a "soldier" for the camorra, which had tightened its grip on Naples after the earthquake of 1980, to better consolidate control over the massive flow of both drugs and construction funds that were transforming the urban economy. His first assignment was to extort money from a local jeweler. The jeweler balked and managed to hold him until the police arrived. Since his case came up just as public outrage over camorra violence was reaching its peak, Ciro was given the maximum sentence. But as I listened to the Signora, I wondered whether his long prison term was a misfortune or an opportunity. The camorra was reputed to send monthly stipends to the families of its fallen or captive heroes.

"Yeah, we spent six grand on the lawyer, but the judge's hands were tied. Anyway, I have to go to Poggioreale every Thursday, to bring him his meals." With evident pride, Elena told me of the culinary treasures that were to be found in these weekly food baskets. I didn't wonder that tall, gangly Ciro had put some weight on, but it was hard to imagine him as a gangster. The image of an awkward adolescent boy, slobbering and cowering on his knees beneath the merciless hail of Stefano's blows, came back to me. Ciro had obeyed his father's commandment to swallow his own cries. Now he was a petty commander in the province of fear, a lord of bullies, a fugitive, fled forever from the claims of ordinary guilt.

"How all this trouble must make you suffer, Signora."

"More than that goddamned wife of his, that's for sure! A mother is only a mother, Tommaso." She shrugged her shoulders. It was four o'clock and I thought I should go. Elena reached for a remote control unit and flicked on the television. She explained that a favorite soap opera was

162

coming on, and the tension around her eyes let me know that the time for conversation was over. I rose to go and asked when I might return. She accompanied me to the door and told me that on Friday night there would be a birthday party for the two-year-old son of Ciro, up in the hotel by the stadium where her daughter Nina was living with her husband. Did I know how to get there? Stefano would be expecting me. Everyone would be there: Gennaro, with his wife and kids, and Giuseppe and Robertino.

"Robertino? How is he?"

"He's working, Tommaso, in the leather factory downstairs." She was growing impatient. "He's all grown up now, but he's still terrible. He does the karate, the boxing, you know, what do you call them?"

"You mean, the martial arts? And Pasquale, how is Pasquale, Signora?"

"Better not to speak of that shithead," she replied. "He's in Germany." She glanced back at the TV. "Look, we'll see you tomorrow night, O.K., Tommaso?"

The soccer stadium of Naples is the architectural centerpiece of the outlying satellite district of Fuorigrotta. Like the elevated expressways that wall off the northern perimeters of the city, it appears to have been not so much constructed as excreted from a gigantic and inexhaustible, if concealed, tube of grey cement. In some future time, its ruins will recall, not so much the nearby coliseums and amphitheaters that gave the circus its character and name, but rather the heavy slabs and stark angles of Stonehenge—still bidding for tribal victory on a deserted windswept plain. The second-class hotels that surround the stadium are as drab and as gray as the nearby parking lots and metro stops that likewise serve the needs of the hordes of fans who regularly converge from all over Italy to be part of an ancient ritual of self-obliteration. It was in one of these hotels, in a large but single bedroom with bath,

163

that Nina, the daughter of Stefano and Elena, had begun a new life as the wife of a young man named Nello. Her wedding present from Stefano was the room itself. In the chaotic aftermath of the earthquake of 1980, it was to this hotel room that Stefano and his entire family had been assigned, until new emergency housing could be built in the suburbs for Naples' homeless thousands. But when, to Stefano's dismay, Fontana del Re was reclassified as safe, he transferred the precious (rent-free) hotel room to Nina.

Arriving at the entrance of the hotel early on Friday evening, I was directed by some teenagers in the lobby to the third floor. The hallways were covered with grafitti and poorly lit, since no one had replaced the burnt-out bulbs that hung in single file along the ceiling. Scanning the corridors, I came across the name of Stefano scrawled at odd angles onto the door. I knocked. The door opened and I was pulled inside by a short hairy unshaven man in navy blue shorts and a sleeveless T-shirt who scowled at me and grinned.

"Tommaso, what a scoundrel you are for not having come to see us sooner." His features had not changed. Rather, it was as though the passing years had sandblasted all remaining traces of youthful softness from his face to expose the jagged bedrock below. Stefano immediately seated me at a rickety folding table. I had arrived just as supper was about to be served. There wasn't very much space, since between the dining table and the double bed, the room was almost full. Elena, Nina, and another young woman came out of the bathroom that had somehow been converted into a makeshift kitchen. Each was bearing a bowl of rigatoni with meat sauce. Nina was 8 months pregnant and as she approached to embrace me, she bobbed from side to side. Her large soft almond eyes were still those of an adolescent girl, but her nose had thickened and her

164

mouth and chin were pressing closer together. Soon, she would be Elena's twin.

Stefano's first-born son, Gennaro, appeared at the doorway with a plain-looking woman rendered all the more plain by her bright red lipstick. Two well-scrubbed toddlers stood at attention at her side. He cut across the room and stared at me, incredulous at my appearance.

"God, it is ugly when we age." He was genuinely horrified, as though I had just been tricked into crossing a magical, if accursed, boundary, and had grown old, bent, and wizened in an instant before his very eyes.

"Yes, Gennaro," I sighed, trying to hide my annoyance as I hugged him, "the years have been too cruel—to us all!" I glanced downward at his ballooning paunch. But he seemed not to understand. He took me aside and told me that he had become a very religious man in recent years. He had become disillusioned first with the Communists, through whom he had obtained his job as a garbage man, and then with the Fascists, whose honesty he was beginning to doubt. Now, with the help of a local priest, he was acquiring the ability to heal the sick and to exorcize devils. Since I wrote about such things, perhaps I would like to hear more about his new career. He gave me his address and phone number and extracted a promise that I would call him within the week. His father-in-law had found him a rent-controlled apartment in the old quarter of run-down palaces and winding lanes known as Sanità. When I asked him about the whereabouts of his brothers, Pasquale and Pepe, he said, "Not now, Tommaso, not here."

I did not at first recognize the tall sandy-haired young man who extended his hand to me with smiling embarrassed eyes before sitting at my side. One eye was ringed with a halo of purple. He rejected the bowl of pasta that Elena set in front of him. She took it away obediently and

165

returned with a half-portion. He sat beside me in silence and ate reluctantly with an indolent and aloof grace. His lightly bronzed skin and golden hair, so stylishly cut, seemed somehow out of place here, amid the harsh animal sounds that his father and brother were making as they ate. I thought of Donatello's Perseus, Mann's Tadziu, *The Prince and the Pauper*. Could this golden dusky-eyed young man be Robertino, the menace, racing round the table, broomstick in hand, ready to pounce and crack? And if so, is he as inscrutable and as self-possessed as he seems?

Stefano must have read my thoughts. "Rob e sempre terribile, Tommaso. (He is as bad as ever!) You should see him with his boxing gloves on. So what if he's a lightweight. He'll be a great champion someday. We hope anyway."

"So that's how you got that black eye, Rob? Sparring?"

"No, no, Tommaso, I had to give Robertino a good beating." Stefano voice was subdued, double-edged with regret and pride.

"His dear old papa still has to give him a good beating once in a while. Doesn't he Rob?" Stefano laughed and poked his index finger into his hollow cheek, teasing Rob, pleading for a kiss.

Elena nodded, "You should see him on the street, Tommaso!" admonishing me to believe in her son's reputation for ferocity. In one arm, she held a platter of fried smelts. In the other, a squirming baby boy.

"This is Ciro's boy, Tommaso, and this is the wife." I was not told her name. She was pale and homely. She puzzled at me through a cloud of cigarette smoke and squinted. The baby, by contrast, was bouncy and curious. He reached out to me, but whether to caress or deliver a smack, I could not tell. He looked very much like his father, with rough-cut features that impressed me as being prematurely masculine. Interrupting my half-hearted at-

166

tempt to amuse the baby, Nello, the young husband of Nina, scooped him up out of his grandmother's arms and tossed and swung him through the air, shouting and exclaiming. The baby was thrilled, hushed with pleasure. Nello passed him to Robertino, who tickled and teased him, before Nina took him up and danced around the bed, cooing at him and laughing, covering him, head to toe, with lingering kisses. How he accepted her adoration! His eyes rolled backward. "Lucky kid," I thought, "to be able to experience so completely the sheer infantile ecstacy of total physical surrender."

Working together silently, the four women cleared the table quickly, carrying dishes and silverware into the bathroom. Elena ordered us into the hallway outside, where, to my surprise, at least a dozen people had gathered on a landing near the stairwell. Stefano had set up a folding table, some beach chairs, and a small bar of sorts, with a bottle of festive Scotch, a case of spumante, and an ice bucket. Nello was running an extension cord to a small record player. Elena appeared, arms extended to display her offering of a large round yellow layer cake. It sagged to one side, giving away its homemade origins. It had been generously iced with thick brushstrokes—all waves and crests—of a rich fudgy chocolate frosting. Two brave little red candles burned away—and waved their pennants of yellow blue-green fire. Robertino held the baby close to the cake while "Happy Birthday" was sung. Nello took deep breaths, to show the boy how to blow out the candles. The child's face beamed bright with joy. He understood. He puffed and sputtered mightily at the flames, causing them some minor inconvenience. But before they could regain their poise, Nello finished them off and the crowd burst into clapping. Two young men, neighbors from the floor, shook bottles of spumante and uncorked them. Holding them at the groin, they hosed the rest of us down

167

and doubled up with laughter. Suddenly the space was filled with the record player's blaring scratchy music, baleful tones of a strong female vocalist, singing in dialect a song that was neither folk nor rock. Some of the teenaged girls began to dance with one another. Nina came over to me and presented me with the gift of a phonograph record, a 45. The company name was "HIT'S." The title was in Neapolitan dialect, 'E Ddoie Mamme (Two Moms). The photo on the envelope pictured a shapely, long-legged young woman (Nina) dressed in tight jeans and high beige vinyl boots, clinging desperately to an older woman, also wearing high beige vinyl boots, while another older woman, more traditionally dressed, reached toward the girl with open pleading arms. The singer's name was printed at the bottom, Nina Bionda. Nina gave me a brief synopsis of the complex plot contained in the song, a psychodrama that explored the contradictions and limitations inherent in a purely biological concept of motherhood.

"So, Nina, when will you cut your next record?"

She sighed deeply "It costs, Tommaso, it costs."

"You're talking five or six grand for an album," Elena shouted over the din. "But for the career of Nina Bionda, it's worth it."

"Do you still get a lot of work singing at weddings?" I asked, remembering that, a few years back, Stefano, had, in effect, given up his moving work to become the booking agent for his daughter, confident in her future as a star entertainer.

"No, Tommee, Nello goes out on the singing jobs by himself now. I have to stay home." I stared dumbly at her big belly and wondered why she had chosen to call me "Tommee." Perhaps it was show business chic to use diminutives. Nina waved her arm toward the dressing table. Three shiny silver trophies on black plastic mounts and two smaller plaques were arranged beside a vase of plastic

168

flowers. All were inscribed with her name. When I congratulated her as sincerely as I knew how, Nina bowed her head, tenderly and with gratitude. I knew then that she had no illusions concerning "La Carrièra di Nina Bionda." Then I recalled the crisis that her outstanding grades in school had once caused her family. One of her teachers had even visited Stefano and Elena to plead with them to send her on to an academic high school, in preparation for a university education. That was when Stefano had bought that illustrated encyclopedia from a traveling salesman, as a token of his recognition and appreciation of Nina's scholastic gifts. But no daughter of his was going to become a university *puttana,* screwing around with whomever and spouting all that rich kid's radical horseshit. So it was that the five-volume encyclopedia, with its imitation black leather binding and gold-painted roman numerals had become yet another forgotten artifact in the archaeology of a workman's household. The whole family gathered round when, months later, after dinner, I asked if I might see it. The notion that it might enter the profane and practical domain of useful objects was a source of amusement and wonder. Stefano's hospitality was boundless.

"Go ahead, Tommaso, read! Read all you want. You'll be the first one in this house to crack that book!"

But the powerfully built woman and mother-to-be facing me now was not one to fondle faded desires. For all her frustrated creative and intellectual potentials, I could not see her as a victim. Perhaps Nina had *chosen* her life, chosen to locate the ground of her being in relationships as opposed to abstractions? Nello joined us. Grimly, he placed a glossy album in my hand, with a movie star photo of his handsome nineteen-year-old face that showed him leaning back, languorous and yearning. By contrast, the young man now talking to me was jumpy, restless, and tense, with a clenched angry cast to his jaw. He played the record and monitored my reaction. I wondered whether I was praising it too much for its "professional" sound? No, Nello was pleased. Would I bring the record to the Feast of San Gennaro when I returned to New York and convince the organizers to play it just once? Nina mumbled something about working with her father on the truck and Nello turned to me, indignant and protesting.

"Do you think a skinny little guy like me is cut out for that kind of heavy work? Look at me, look at my arms." He pinched a perfectly respectable, if rather flaccid, bicep. He was a short, slight, but undeniably wiry man, with silky black hair and graceful, dark, almost feline features. Without any reliable source of income of his own, Stefano was probably supporting him. I even wondered whether he had been forced, under pressure, to marry Nina.

"I swear Tommaso, the penis is the worst thing a man has . . . It's the worst thing on this earth! Look what kind of trouble it can get you into." He glanced resentfully at the bulge in Nina's middle. He was genuinely distressed. Elena placed a dish of cake in front of him, as though to placate him and offer her sympathy. But our conversation was stopped abruptly in its tracks by the sound of a man gasping. A frightful, cracking scream escaped like a struggling demon from the depths of Stefano's open twisting mouth.

"Oh my God!" Elena shrieked. The baby boy had found a wall outlet and was trying to insert any finger that would fit into the socket. He seemed nonplussed by his grandfather's by now ear-splitting hollering and went on with his careful, methodical probing. But Elena seized the child in the nick of time and swept him up off the floor. She held him close to her bosom, as he pouted and readied himself to cry. I thought Stefano would faint with relief. I too was stunned, shaken by the alarm and dramatic rescue. Elena

170

cuddled the boy. Then she looked at me quizzically. Her expression turned sad and serene.

"This baby is a deaf mute, Tommaso. You didn't know, did you?" She handed the child to his mother. For the first time that evening, I heard the baby's hoarse panting cry. But then someone turned on the music and soon we were all dancing and drinking glass after glass of that cheap but sweet, effervescent spumante. Then, out of nowhere, Nello appeared in clownish drag, with a blonde wig, rouged cheeks, a flaring pillow-stuffed bottom, and two Jaffa grapefruits for breasts. When he pursed his ruby-red lips, and began a ridiculous—because so clumsy—bump and grind striptease, everyone split their sides laughing. Nello kept the crowd clapping with a lurid ribald song, something having to do with "u pacche sorride" (your sister's ass), sung with great comic skill. By now, at least thirty people had gathered on the landing, drinking and laughing. When Nello's remarkable can-can performance was finished, everyone cheered.

I wondered. "Was this the same angry little tough guy, who, a few minutes ago, had been dreaming aloud his futile Frank Sinatra dreams and complaining so bitterly about the bonds of marriage and fatherhood? And where was he, *who* was he now?"

Here, I realized, winking and leering before me, was the ancient god-king of Naples. Forget San Gennaro, with his heavy silver treasure and church-managed ritual of bubbling ceremonial blood. In this bleak concrete bunker of a welfare hotel, in this smoggy haze of mind-dulling heat on a late twentieth-century evening in July, I had witnessed the resurrection of the spirit of Pulcinella himself, the long-nosed, rooster-clown who can see all the forms of the soul in black and white at once—sly trickster, equalizer and killer; strutting cock and flaming fairy, farting his

171

way to infamy and letting the air out of all the world's stuffed shirts and over-inflated balloons.

And what of the child who could not hear his own Happy Birthday song? What to make of that? Was he cut off from the rest of us by our knowledge of his predicament, no longer a cooing babe but a crippled dwarf fated to become a paranoid hermit, isolated forever in a prison cell of absolute impenetrable silence? He never heard the champagne popping or the stereo playing the songs of his aunt Nina and her would-be crooner of a husband. But how he had relished his grandma's good cake and gotten himself all mustachioed with fudge. How he had tottered and stumbled about, like a drunken shrunken Charlie Chaplin, after his second gulp of spumante. When Elena offered him her cigarette, he had sucked at it hungrily and breathlessly, to savor the rare pleasure of smoking. And recall how he had carried different household objects about to organize a circle of exchange from person to person, presenting and then taking away—clothespins, ashtrays, cups, utensils, crayons. These were his toys, and his gifts of appeasement.

"Won't he have to go to a special institute, Signora? Maybe I could find out about it for you."

"Someday, Tommaso. We've taken him to all the specialists. When he gets older, there's some kind of school for the deaf. Stefano knows where it is." I was scandalized by her nonchalance, but on my way home later that evening I realized that Ciro's son would probably fare better in the cramped second-class hotel rooms and the glass-strewn playing fields of Fuorigrotta than in the gleaming corridors of some state-run institute. Here, he will grow up knowing more in his silence than he would in a place that could equip him with the prostheses of communication, but exclude him from that country of love and sor-

172

row where the family of Stefano and Elena make their permanent home.

My visit with Stefano's family left me gratified and relieved. After all, didn't they treat me as though I belonged in their midst? In some ways, didn't they regard me as a member of their family? In their presence, and especially in Stefano's presence, I felt less alone, less exploitative, and thus less of a stranger. Although I wasn't always sure whether the Signora wanted me around, Stefano's warm welcoming embrace and complete lack of pretense reversed the outward, flight-prone directionality of my mind. I gazed, not toward the airport and the jet that would return me to that illusion of a refuge that I called home, but inward. I lifted my head up to the new home, and to the new life, to the fresh start and the more heroic identity that I might make for myself in Naples.

In the weeks that followed, I was able to renew my "Sunday dinner" relationship with Stefano and his family. Life in Stefano's household was calmer now. The violent quarrels of previous years had subsided. The Signora's meals were just as elaborate and labor-intensive as before but they were more often consumed in silence as everyone gazed at the TV. No one program seemed to command their attention for very long. Stefano was constantly switching channels as though anything would be preferable to watching one hated commercial through to completion. Only the Japanese cartoons, with their simple violent plots documenting a boy-hero's victory over some sinister world-destroyer, could stop the frantic channel-changing. Local channels that featured Neapolitan singers and variety shows were watched with a kind of playful and participatory glee as though the performers were family intimates. Aside from the soap operas, the "serious" programs rarely claimed the screen for more than a few seconds. But it was food and babies that still held stage center in Elena's family. I recall one such Sunday afternoon in the fall of 1984. Stefano had taken Pepe with him on a moving job in earthquake-racked Pozzuoli nearby. Upon returning, Stefano washed quickly, and sat at the table to be served. His facial bones were more gaunt than usual, his black darting eyes more crazed. I realized that, for Stefano, the interval between work-time and meal-time was fraught with a tension that only his wife's food could allay. Pepe, by contrast, was lethargic and bored, obviously demoralized by a Sunday morning spent at hard labor. He barely managed to greet me with a sullen smile.

Nina and Nello arrived with their six month old baby boy. A pregnant young woman, stylishly dressed, with jet-black hair and large white teeth, accompanied them. I later learned that she was one of Nello's two sisters. He had eighteen brothers, each with a reputation more infamous than the next! I assumed, therefore, that the woman was either married or widowed. A yawning Robertino appeared and sat quietly beside his sister. While Nina fed her baby some mashed bananas, the Signora served bowls of linguini with a fresh white clam sauce, then a second course of stuffed roasted fish, and finally a third course of fried fish accompanied by chilled red peppers. As she cleared my empty plate, she bellowed at me, "I can throw a little something together every now and then, no, Tommaso?" Desserts had attained a prominence that I did not recall from the previous decade. Homemade creampuffs with chocolate sauce were followed by cups of fresh fruit, marinated in a sweet lemon liqueur and topped with whipped cream. Finally, a large tray of nuts and fruit appeared. Stefano seized an orange and summarily sliced it in half. He dumped a tablespoon of sugar onto both halves. Drenching each in whiskey, he shouted at me, almost

174

vengefully, "It's not only the rich who know how to eat well, Tommaso!" I tried not to notice as the drunken orange exploded between his teeth, spurting liquor and sugary juices down his whiskered chin onto the tablecloth below.

Nina's baby was already obese. She told me that the doctor had warned her not to feed him too much. Elena cooed and fussed over him in terms that I had never heard before:

"Do you want to be your grandma's little drag queen?" (in dialect: "Vuó essere 'o fumaniello d'à nonna?")

"No, nonna," protested Nello's sister as she took the infant into her arms. She laughed gently, in tones of mock indignation, and in her own husky, sensual voice, defended his imperiled masculine pride, "I'm a man and I want to be a man." But Elena was undaunted. She replied that the day before she had seen a little girl's dress for a hundred bucks in a shop-window.

"It was so pretty. I wanted to dress *him* up in it." She sighed wistfully. Clearly for her, the expression of possessive maternal desire was a vital component of its gratification.

After dinner, Stefano's son, Gennaro, dropped by and I found myself caught in a double conversation. On the one side was Nello, the natural performer, elfin and sprightly now in his joke-telling mode. Nello's jokes were vulgar, grotesque and hilarious in the ancient Saturnalian sense. In each, a weak point in the theory and praxis of conventional morality was referred to a comparable weak point in the genito-urinary and gastro-intestinal tracts of the human body. On my other side was Gennaro, who, though he could not control his laughter at Nello's Rabelaisian humor, was urgently recounting to me his adventures as an exorcist. From a priest renowned in Naples for his skill at casting out demons, Gennaro had learned the

175

rudiments of the technique. The demon's presence was always made manifest in laughter, and so it was necessary first to incite from the victim the devil's frightful laughter and only then to intone the requisite explosive incantations. But because Gennaro had declared himself an avowed enemy of the evil one, he was himself now the victim of the latter's nightly visitations. By holding tightly to his wife's hand, however, he could overcome his awful fear and permit himself to sleep. Nello and I were soon sobered by Gennaro's grim stories of satanic possession and laughter. As though to reassure Gennaro of whose side he was on, Nello described a song that he had recently written and performed, called "La Buca." It was a ballad that celebrated the progress of a young drug addict who was able to renounce his addiction after seeing a picture of the madonna. With the assistance and support of the person dearest to him, he kicked the habit for good and held down a steady job. In Naples, of course, this dearest person is neither a girlfriend, nor a wife, nor a comrade but always, the one and only, "Mama."

It was after Pepe, Robertino and Gennaro had left that Nina asked me whether Pepe had borrowed any money from me of late. When I told her that I had helped him out with some minor loans, she alluded to his drug problem. Not sure of how much I already knew, she mentioned some pills that they had found in his pockets. I told her that he had been honest with me about his addiction. But when I tried to persuade Stefano that the boy desperately needed treatment, he broke his tight-lipped silence. Slamming his fist against the tabletop, he vowed to have Pepe committed to an insane asylum for life if he didn't shape up soon. It was clear that the discussion was closed. Nina accompanied me to the door, warning me not to help her brother anymore, while with her eyes she implored me to help him all I could.

176

Epilogue: Return to Naples

In the course of my visits to Stefano and Elena, I occasionally mentioned, in passing, the book about Naples that I had written. But discussion usually foundered on their amusement at its title, which, in Italian, sounds like "The Broken Sink." "Tommaso's become a plumber. Bravo, bravo!" At one point during my stay, I was interviewed by the city's leading newspaper. The feature appeared with a large photograph of me on the second page. The publicity changed my relationship to the people of Fontana del Re in ways that I could not have imagined. Initially, I was told, the sight of the photograph triggered a reaction of surprise and sympathy. "They got Tommaso!" went the rumor. "He was one of us all along."

Impatient with the slow and somewhat redundant pace of participant observation, I thought that the fame that attended my newspaper interview could be turned to good account in my research. Stefano had flatly refused my earlier request for his life history. "My life story would read like a novel, Tommaso," he assured me, "but I'll go to my grave with it." I wasn't sure whether, in refusing, he was guarding his privacy or trying to prevent the contamination of our friendship by instrumental motives that he located outside the circle of familial intimacy to which he had granted me admittance. Maybe now I could convince him, and likewise Elena, to change their minds and help me with my new project.

But I was still left with the problem of my submerged identity as a fieldworker. On my next visit, a few nights later, I brought along a copy of *The Broken Fountain*. Stefano was both mystified and impressed. What could I possibly have written about? Had I made any money on the book? When I explained that it was intended for a limited readership composed largely of professors, students, and the like, he seemed relieved. The Signora frowned impatiently.

177

"Next time, make a movie, Tommaso. There's no money in books, not for you and not for us!" Stefano was eager to know what part dealt with him and with his family. Would I find the pages and translate them into Italian? I read some passages dealing with Robertino and everyone seemed delighted. Robertino blushed. They were all genuinely awed that an entire chapter had been devoted to them. But they were disturbed as well. Nina gave voice to everyone's worst fears.

"Did you say anything about Pasquale in the book?"

"Yes."

"Did you write about when he took the poison and had to be hospitalized?"

"Yes."

The Signora nodded, knowingly, as though she had never expected more from me in the first place. But Stefano would be the judge now. The tone of his response would determine hers. Stefano's eyes were cast down toward the table. I saw that he was ashamed for both of us. Although I had told him long ago that I had come to Naples to write about his way of life, it was clear that he had not expected *his* life to be held up to the world's scrutiny. I recalled how he had once warned me to guard against the possibility of his eventual betrayal of our friendship. I had issued no such warning.

"Well, Tommaso, they haven't translated it into Italian yet, have they?"

"No, Stefano. It won't be translated. Outside of Naples, in Rome, Florence, or Milan, people think they know all there is to know about Naples. You know what I mean? And here in Naples, who would want to read a book about the things they see and hear every day." The Signora seemed satisfied and surprised. I had said something sensible.

"Tommaso is right. After all, who would shell out good

money to read about our ordinary lives? Americans maybe, but to Americans, we Neapolitans aren't ordinary. Let *me* tell you the truth about Neapolitans, Tommaso. They stink. Always trying to get something for nothing and nobody wants to work."

As I tried to dismiss the appeal and importance of the book by explaining cultural anthropology's concern with the boring and inconsequential trivia of daily, domestic, and even private life, Stefano gave the book to Elena to put away or rather, to hide. Nina brought me a cool wet towel. My throat was dry. My heart had been beating wildly and I was drenched in sweat. Gradually, my breathing returned to normal. I felt like a prisoner suddenly set free from a high-powered lie detector that had gone haywire whenever I protested, "I was only doing my job." The Signora placed a dish of breaded cutlets and curling slivers of fried eggplant in front of me. After a few glasses of a harsh and soda-like *Lambrusco* wine, Stefano shook his finger and scolded me gently.

"You are a little bit of a liar, aren't you, Tommaso." There wasn't a trace of anger in his voice. Rather, like a wise and caring teacher, he wanted to grant me this small, but precious gift of critical self-knowledge. After a few more glasses of the anomalous *Lambrusco,* Stefano grew drowsy and I said goodnight.

The next morning, I went searching for my old friend, Eduardo, nicknamed "Il Saggio" (the Wise Man). I knew that, after the earthquake of 1980, he had "occupied" an empty apartment in the Quattro Palazzi district and had refused to pay rent, claiming squatter's rights. I found him toward noon sleeping on a rumpled bed, surrounded by overloaded ashtrays and reeking, empty beercans. Apparently, he had fallen asleep fully dressed, in jeans and a T-shirt. On an upturned crate beside the bed was a pad of lined writing paper, some envelopes, and a few crumpled pages covered with Eduardo's labored, careful handwriting. The overhead light was on, despite the fact that the room was flooded with sunlight. The front door had been left ajar. Screwed to the door was a rather elegant plaque inscribed with Eduardo's full name. I called out to him. He did not waken and I hesitated to disturb him. I drew closer. Even as he slept, his brow was furrowed, drawn together and knitted over the bridge of his thin, still delicate nose. His forehead was already grooved with the unmistakeable penknife incisions of chronic worry. The stubble on his unshaven face was patchy, with glints of silver, but overall his features had retained their boyish cast and their classical, Pompeian lines.

Upon waking he expressed no real surprise to see me. As he explained over the can of cold beer that he fetched as soon as he got out of bed, the rumor had been out for some time that I was an undercover cop living in Caserta (a suburb), who reappeared in Naples periodically to investigate the camorra and the drug trade. Since the economy of Fontana del Re had been given a powerful boost in the past decade by the employment opportunities that had been created by the demand for cocaine, I wondered whether Eduardo's casual comment meant that I might be in danger. But Eduardo had already forgiven me my deceit. He was glad to see me again.

"You know I've been doing a lot of writing myself lately, Tommaso." He laughed, "I don't understand why, but I'm writing letters to all my friends. Last night, I nailed a whole stack of letters to the doors of the University." I asked Eduardo if I could see some of the letters. The first one that he showed me was addressed to a mutual acquaintance, a doctor who had once befriended him. It was garbled and fragmented, with numerous and often angry references to prostitutes and venereal disease. It began with

180

a request for a loan, but the major theme concerned the sudden death of Eduardo's mother of a heart attack five years before. Eduardo had apparently never recovered from the loss. All of the letters that I subsequently read were essentially the same. The request for a loan from a higher status male was followed by a frankly sexual expression of rage toward his widowed and deceased mother (identified now as a source of infection and death) and a closing reference to the "beautiful cock that Eduardo wants to give to all of your pretty students and schoolteachers." Reading these letters, I realized why so many people at Fontana del Re had been embarrassed by my questions concerning the whereabouts of Eduardo. Eduardo's illness did not serve to reassure those who knew him of their essential sanity. His was rather a cautionary tale, a Neapolitan gloss on the Sermon on the Mount: "Accursed are the meek, for they shall go mad."

In the weeks that followed, I tried to piece together the shards of the vessel that had been Eduardo's personality. In the late spring of 1975, in the weeks immediately following my departure from Naples, Eduardo had participated in the street riots of the Disoccupati Organizzati (the union of the unemployed). This remarkable but short-lived organization had arisen spontaneously among the chronically unemployed of the city around the rallying cry of jobs for all. Eduardo endured a brutal beating at the hands of the police. His myriad black and blue badges of revolutionary courage eventually qualified him for a job as "gardener" in a small park near the Royal Palace. The new Communist administration that came to power in Naples on the shoulders of the Disoccupati saw to it that he received approximately $400.00 per month. All that was required of him and the sixty others now on the gardening staff (of a three acre park) was to sign in every weekday morning. Since the foreman of the crew also signed in and disappeared, Eduardo was not able to work even on the days when he felt inclined to do so. To insist upon his right to work, he assured me, would invite immediate dismissal. He had wanted to plant some flowers in the gardens, but there were no flowers to be found and the tool shed was locked.

Eduardo passed a few hours every afternoon in the company of his mother, who sold contraband cigarettes out of a storefront at Fontana del Re. His mother was a heavy-set, quiet woman with gentle eyes and a restful reassuring manner. Normally gregarious and tense, Eduardo was silent and at peace in his mother's presence. When his mother died suddenly, Eduardo roamed the streets of downtown Naples, weeping out loud, raving and mumbling incoherently. In the weeks after her burial, he began to have his first terrifying x-ray visions. He no longer saw the people around him in the flesh. He saw only their skeletons and, not surprisingly, he recoiled in terror and fled. In Campo Santo, the cemetery of Naples, the death rituals of the ancient Mediterranean world—with their prescribed exhumations, inspections, and reburials of the decayed or miraculously preserved corpse—had only recently fallen into disuse. I wondered whether the form of Eduardo's psychosis did not reflect his memory of these lapsed funerary traditions.

Eduardo was hospitalized for six months, placed on medication and released. His sister invited him to live with her and her children. Because her husband had left her, Eduardo took upon himself the role of watchdog and guardian of her chastity. Whether based on paranoia or genuine moral outrage, their arguments and clashes grew progressively more severe. The earthquake of 1980 aggravated his morbid obsession with death, but it also presented him with an opportunity to escape his sister's household. He located and claimed an uninhabited apartment in a drab tenement near the Central Station. The owners of this apartment lived next door. They were not pleased with the young squatter who took up residence (temporarily but legally, as a homeless earthquake victim) in the apartment that they were warehousing, in hopes of fetching a high black market rent. Eduardo feuded and argued almost daily with his owner-neighbors and on one occasion came to blows. The police were called and he was taken in for questioning. In 1983 his condition began to deteriorate again. A few weeks before my arrival, he had mounted the rooftop of the building at midnight to tell the world of his carnal attractions and intentions toward "all the schoolteachers of Naples," exhibiting the signs and singing the praises of his ardor. But apparently, for Eduardo, this desperate affirmation of desire could only be resolved in an excess of blind rage. As a grand finale to his amorous declarations, he hauled his precious new Sony television set and washing machine onto and over the side of the balcony and gleefully watched them crash to the cobblestones eight flights below.

What knotted cord of gut-level experience, I asked myself, might lead a handsome young man like Eduardo to focus his sexual desires on a slum child's prim and proper schoolteachers? How might Freud have accounted for all this frenzied oedipal thrashing in a tightening, confining net of class hatred, envy, and the desire to possess and destroy? If Marx was right in claiming that commodities are never mere objects but rather fetishes invested with spiritual potency, then what religion did Eduardo seek to desecrate with his ritual sacrifice of a washing machine? Finally, why would a lonely and contemplative man plead for shared understanding and friendship in the denigrating idiom of countless petty cash loans? Indeed, as I spent more and more time with Eduardo in the ensuing weeks, his requests for small amounts of money became more frequent and burdensome. So often, in fact, did he ask me for money that I began to estimate the probable cost of meeting him beforehand.

In the early autumn of 1983 Eduardo and I met each other daily, to take long walks along the sea. Eduardo liked to sit on an outcropping of rock that commanded a grand view of Vesuvius and the bay. Our conversations were both gravely and preposterously philosophical, as Eduardo framed his questions from his customary position of an innocence that was as sincere as it was absolute.

"What happens after we die, Tommaso? Why do we die? How do you live knowing you're going to die?"

"How do you get women? I want a woman, Tommaso. Give me some tips . . . No, but I just want to lie back. I want her to do all the work."

"My mother was a filthy whore, Tommaso. She fucked, didn't she?"

"When you put your money in a bank, Tommaso, what does the bank do with it? What happens to the money?"

"Tommaso, do you think that the pigeons have feelings like we do? When I was a boy, I would look for the ones with broken wings and take them home and fix them up. But my brother would find them and roast them for lunch."

"Shit, my front teeth are falling out! Tommaso, why don't you make yourself useful for once and help me find a toothpaste that works, a toothpaste that really works! Let's go to the drug store. By the way, could you lend me, say, twenty?"

Eduardo was suspended from his job in mid-October for failing to sign the morning register. He made no attempt to reinstate himself. Instead, he befriended a group of barefoot young panhandlers who slept in the waiting rooms of the Central Station and invited them to his place. Eduardo provided the extra mattresses and the beer and they provided the guitar music and the girls. His requests for money became more onerous than ever and I began to debate the wisdom of acceding to his demands. In Eduardo's eyes, I was wealthy and wise, with access to vast but mysterious structures of knowledge and power that he both hated and desired. Just as he could no longer mediate the polarities that normally separate the maternal and the erotic aspects of woman, neither could he keep the domains of the market and the gift in their proper cultural cages. If I turned him down, I would wound him and probably lose him. Once more, I was forced to wrestle with the problem of my own anthropological venality. After all, as a fieldworker, I too worked with categories that leaked. How valuable was Eduardo to my research? If I really cared about keeping him as my friend, shouldn't I have aired my feelings and stopped the loans immediately?

In early December Eduardo set to work on a *"presepe,"* a traditional Neapolitan Christmas manger. He collected all sorts of decorations and figurines and built a miniature stable and a papier-mâché rock formation in hopes of re-creating a landscape that would befit the miracle of the virgin birth. When it was finished, he painted a sign to designate the scene. It read "Il Buono Natale" (The Good Christmas). Eduardo was proud of his work and boasted that his *presepe* was "the best and most elaborate in all of Naples." He invited his new friends from the station to admire the manger and to celebrate the holiday with him. I was persuaded to shed my Scrooge image and loan him even more money as he shopped for a grand Christmas Eve feast. In his absence, some of Eduardo's guests burglarized the apartment of his landlord. They deposited the stolen merchandise (a stereo and a TV) in Eduardo's apartment. These were identified to the police by a relieved and delighted landlord. Upon returning home, Eduardo was arrested and accused of the crime. He spent

185

his Christmas in a holding cell. A month later, he was convicted of petit larceny and sent to Poggioreale, the infamous prison of Naples, for a term of one year. At his trial, he outraged the judge by repeatedly interrupting the proceedings with loud exclamations of his innocence. "But, Judge," he shouted in dialect, "I didn't do anything wrong!" The public prosecutor referred to him as "a confused and lost young man, from an environment and a *culture* very different from our own." He went on to demand appropriate punishment. The lawyer that his older brother and I had retained did not speak up in Eduardo's defense. I suspected that the deal that he had tried to work out beforehand with the judge had been sabotaged by Eduardo's protests. Only later did I learn that a plea of guilty had been entered and that an insanity defense would have risked a mandatory minimum sentence of two years, no matter whether the offense were murder or shoplifting. Eduardo's brother was pleased with the sentence.

"Oh, it's not so bad, Tommaso. When he's inside, he'll compare his sentence with those who have three, five, and ten years and realize he got off easy. He'll be just fine in Poggioreale. He'll meet up with the old crowd from Fontana del Re."

Soon after Eduardo's trial, I went to see another lawyer, Clara C., a woman renowned in Naples as a fighter for the rights of the poor. I wanted to know whether Eduardo's role as an assistant in my research might form the basis of an appeal. Clara was optimistic but Eduardo would first have to agree to her appointment as his attorney.

Clara was very different from most of the legal professionals whom I had met in Naples. She was vital, compassionate, and intellectually alive. Her speech exhibited none of the ornate rhetorical flourishes that caused so many discussions and arguments to sink of their own verbal weight. I told her of Eduardo's summary and absurd dismissal from

186

a job at which he had never been permitted to work in the first place. She knew the youth employment law under which he had been hired and explained that it was never meant to provide gainful employment but was rather a disguised form of welfare. Imprisonment was far more expensive. The state would pay upwards of $120 a day to keep Eduardo in jail. I described the trial as best I could, telling her of Eduardo's outbursts and the prosecution's attempt to convict him on the basis of his membership in an alien culture. Clara then recounted a recent criminal case in which she had been involved. The case concerned a young woman who had lived in the *Campi Containers,* the cramped trailer camps near the zoo and the amusement park that had been set up by the government to temporarily house thousands of earthquake victims.

The young woman murdered her stepfather, a jovial vendor of cotton candy who worked in the amusement park nearby. How? She strangled him with her nylon stockings. Then, with a broken bottle, she disemboweled him, removed his intestines and his heart, and draped them decorously round his limp neck. She showed no signs of guilt. Rather, she accused the old man of maligning her chastity.

During the trial, it was revealed that the deceased was a brutal and cruel man who had, in all probability, violated his stepdaughter throughout her adolescence. When she became engaged to a young factory worker, her stepfather forced her to make a tape in which she expressed a sexual preference for old men. When she announced her intention of marrying the young man, he blackmailed her with the tape.

But the most interesting detail of the story concerned a sociolinguistic oddity. When she testified, she claimed that the sight of her stepfather dozing in his easy chair caused her to "insemmai." "M'insemmai!" she cried out in the courtroom. The word "insemmai" is a Neapolitan

187

word with no Italian root that means "to go out of one's mind." The judge, when he wrote up his decision against her, used the Neapolitan term. "At that moment," he wrote, "the girl 'insemmaied.'" According to Clara, this was a clever way of dismissing the validity of her testimony, as well as the legitimacy of the insanity defense. The fact that the young woman had described her emotional state—crucial to the verdict—in her own native language of emotion was her undoing. She could have no clemency as long as she testified in dialect.

Clara advised me as to what kind of letters I might write to facilitate Eduardo's appeal. I also wrote to Eduardo in jail, notifying him of Clara's interest in his case. Shortly after our discussion, Clara visited Eduardo. Afterwards, she informed me that the situation was hopeless. At their meeting, Eduardo was disoriented and incredulous. He mistook her for a meddlesome social worker and treated her as such. Apparently, he could not believe that an attractive young woman could be a lawyer in Naples.

I wrote to Eduardo in prison and he responded with a steady stream of letters, sometimes more than one a day. In these letters, he expressed his anger and his anguish but he never gave in to despair. He rarely complained of the physical discomfort that he was enduring. He felt that he had been imprisoned as a direct result of his empathy for others and in his letters he wondered at the temperamental differences that separated him from his peers. He even pointed to the irony of his nickname and pondered its significance. In each of nearly twenty-five letters, he wrote of the rock by the sea where we had groped for the answers to his questions. Here is one of his letters:

Dear Tommaso:

I have thought about your letter so often and I hope that your health is as perfect as the moon that I look up at each night from this cold and damp cell. It is good to know that there are friends who care about me, especially in a place like this, a place I never wanted to see, where there is so much hatred and where one must always be on guard. I want you to know something else very important, that I never committed any crime, that they accused me only so they could kick me out of the home I loved so much, where I suffered so much. I won't let anyone send me away from it again.

I want to tell you so many things Tommaso but unfortunately it's impossible in a place like this. I also want you to know that I only wanted to help those who weren't doing so well in this world. But they didn't take pity on me. They didn't have mercy on me. They got me involved in their crime and they've destroyed my life. But my conscience is as pure as this moon that I'm looking at through these bars and this cement.

I think always of that rock by the sea, Tommaso, where we went together to talk of so many things. My spirit is always close to that rock. The great day will come when I will be free and then we can go together once more to the rock where I thought I had come to understand so many things. But these things weren't of any use to me. But I want news of you, Tommaso. Thus I could feel closer to that wondrous place where the seagulls live, in between a blue sky and a beautiful sun cradled by the waves of the sea. It was there that together we were able to understand so many things.

Write to me right away.
Ciao, Your dear friend,
Eduardo

All of Eduardo's letters invoked the dual symbolism of the rock and the moon and in each he referred to the phases of the changing moon that he could see from his cell. When I thought of him, I saw his troubled face, doe-like, fragile, and moonlit, staring upward through the bars and turning serene. I saw his eyes fill with simple wonder as he sought protection and received it from the ancient goddess with whom, I hoped, he was finally reconciled.

Final Thoughts:
Reflections on Ribera's *The Clubfooted Boy*

Jusepe de Ribera (lo Spagnoletto) painted *The Clubfooted Boy* in 1642 for Don Ramiro Felipe de Guzmán, the viceroy of Naples. The boy was, no doubt, a familiar figure on the streets of Naples. In all probability, he was a *scugnizzo* or street urchin. We can surmise that he was nicknamed after his deformed foot. His surname, if he had one, was most likely "esposito" after "exposed" for "foundling." His teeth and gums are already rotted and his thick dark hair is close-cropped, almost chopped. His clothes are common, but neat and clean. This boy is not malnourished, although his shortened legs and semi-dwarfed appearance hint of earlier nutritional deficiencies. His features are tough, coarse, and masculine and thus very different from the cherubic androgynes favored by Ribera's contemporary, Caravaggio. He is probably nine or ten but he has aged prematurely. His pose is that of a marching soldier and he holds his crutch over his shoulder like a rifle. In his hand is a piece of paper on which are written in Latin the words, "Give me alms for the love of God."

The boy is smiling broadly. His smile is, to say the least, radiant, illumined by and partaking of the sunny light of the billowing sky that forms the background of the painting. He is obviously proud to be the object of the painter's (or is it the viceroy's?) attention. He is unabashedly thrilled to occupy, however briefly, the heroic space of the victorious soldier. In fact, he can hardly contain his joy. He might even be on the verge of laughter.[1]

Ribera's intentions here were neither ethnographic nor political. Working within the confines of aristocratic and ecclesiastical patronage, his genius enabled him to reclaim the artist's ancient role of seer and to probe deep beneath the surface of mere historical time. His crippled laughing boy is an archetypal vision of the wounded healer, of injury and recovery, of decay and rebirth, of dependency and autonomy, and of a plea that is simultaneously a warning and a command.

But in the context of local Western history, Italian history, the history of Naples, the history of palaces and hovels, the history of gluttony and famine, the history of health and disease, the history of freedom and imprisonment, the history of taxation and the dole, the painting is suspect, if only because it brings no small measure of comfort to its owner, the Viceroy, Don Ramiro Felipe de Guzmán.

Representations of human suffering, whether they be oil paintings or ethnographies, that reveal the human capacity for transcendence are likewise suspect if they do not clarify the clouded lenses of pity and terror through which we perceive the sufferer. It is easy enough for the artist to evoke pity at the plight of the victim. It requires a master like Ribera to evoke the grief and the joy, in a word, the sense of atonement that comes from the recognition of the Other as the Same. It is another matter entirely to summon forth, first terror, then outrage, and, finally, meaningful and effective action that is directed toward the identification and removal of the *hidden cause* of the suffering.[2]

The boy in Ribera's painting has been able to defend his essential humanity against great odds. Philosophers and learning theorists can argue as to how. Should we attribute his triumph to his capacity for laughter and his acceptance of the gift of life on any terms, no matter how contingent or harsh? Does his unshaken faith in God and in the generosity of his masters, or, more importantly, in the symbols that legitimate their authority, enable him to trust in the immediate moment and to ask for and expect nothing more than this day's bread? Or is it rather that he

191

took the full measure of power long ago, that he imagined himself to be light as a feather, too light to tip the scales of Justices' massive weights. Accept then the bindings and the constraints. Learn one's helplessness by heart. Be grateful for what is offered. Go lighthearted into Paradise.

When I saw *The Clubfooted Boy* in the Louvre, I defaced it in my mind's eye. Where Esposito stood, I painted Guido in his death agony, stabbed by his pimp or john in some piss-stinking back alley. I painted Pepe, sighing with purest pleasure, as his syringe pumped its magic elixir steady and deep into his swollen vein. I painted Eduardo first with his *presepe* and then behind bars. Lastly, I painted Ciro's deaf mute son smiling through candlelight. For a moment it seemed as though Ribera's vision and mine were one. As the original painting came back into focus, I smiled back at the crippled boy. But my serenity was shattered when I realized that it was not the viceroy now but rather the ethnographer who was enjoying a moment of peace.

notes

Preface

1. The reference is to Yeats' poem, "Among School Children," cited by Kenneth Burke, "Symbolic Action in a Poem by Keats," in *Perspectives by Incongruity*, ed. Stanley Edgar Hyman (Bloomington: Indiana University Press, 1964), p. 138.

2. C. Wright Mills, *The Sociological Imagination* (London: Oxford University Press, 1959), ch. 3.

Introduction: The Broken Fountain in Retrospect

1. James Clifford, "On Ethnographic Authority," in *The Predicament of Culture* (Cambridge: Harvard University Press, 1988), pp. 21–54.

2. D. H. Lawrence, "The Novel," in *Phoenix II: Uncollected Writings,* ed. Warren Roberts and Harry T. Moore (New York: Viking, 1968), pp. 416–26.

3. W. E. B. DuBois, *The Philadelphia Negro: A Social Study* (New York: Schocken, 1967), p. 5.

4. Eric Wolf, "Review of *The Children of Sanchez: Autobiography of a Mexican Family*" in *American Anthropologist,* 70 (1962):620–621. See also, Edward Sapir, "Culture, Genuine and Spurious," in *Culture, Language and Personality,* ed. David G. Mandelbaum (Berkeley: University of California Press, 1949).

5. Sigmund Freud, *Civilization and Its Discontents* (New York: Norton, 1962). On addiction, see especially p. 25.

6. Richard Wright, "How Bigger Was Born," Introduction to *Native Son* (New York: Harper and Row, 1966), p. xix.

7. Robert Jay Lifton, *The Future of Immortality and Other Essays for a Nuclear Age* (New York: Basic Books, 1987), p. 20. On the general cultural significance of the trickster figure, see Paul Radin, *The Trickster: A Study in American Indian Mythology* (New York: Schocken, 1972). On the communicative and paradoxical components of the complex, see Thomas Belmonte, "The Trickster and the Sacred Clown: Revealing the Logic of the Unspeakable," in *C. G. Jung and the Humanities: Toward a Hermeneutics of Culture,* ed. K. Barnaby and P. D'Acierno (Princeton: Princeton University Press, 1989). On the specific permutations of the myth in seventeenth- and eighteenth-century Naples, see John A.

Marino, "Economic Idylls and Pastoral Realities: The 'Trickster' Economy in the Kingdom of Naples," in *Comparative Studies in Society and History*, 24 (1982):211–234.

8. Edmund Carpenter, *Oh, What a Blow that Phantom Gave Me!* (New York: Holt, Rinehart and Winston, 1973).

9. Herbert Gutman, *The Black Family in Slavery and in Freedom, 1750–1925* (New York: Vintage, 1977).

10. Terence Des Pres, *The Survivor: An Anatomy of Life in the Death Camps* (New York, Pocket Books, 1977), p. v.

11. For an excellent study of the economic and political context within which earthquake-damaged working class neighborhoods in Naples were targeted for middle-class renewal or allowed to decline, see Giovanni Laino, *Il Cavallo di Napoli: I Quartieri Spagnoli* (Milano: Franco Angeli Editore, 1984). Judith Chubb has presented a cogent analysis of the role of the housing crisis in Palermo and Naples in fostering popular protest and organization at the neighborhood level, as well as its dissolution in clientelism and political extremism on the Right and the Left. See Judith Chubb, *Patronage, Power, and Poverty in Southern Italy: A Tale of Two Cities* (Cambridge: Cambridge University Press, 1982).

12. The research of Victoria Goddard confirms the indispensable role of women in maintaining group identity in working-class Naples. When economic pressures constrain them to work outside the home, rather than opt for better-paid factory jobs, they typically choose to maximize both familial and patriarchal values in the more exploitative but personalized atmosphere of the neighborhood sweatshop. Moreover in Naples, as in other parts of Italy, whatever psychic trauma attends female adolescence is traditionally focused not on sexuality and parental authority so much as on the crisis of engagement and the attainment of marital and maternal respectability. Maternal power is then consolidated through control over food and the exclusion of males from spheres of domestic competence. Victoria Goddard, "Women's Sexuality and Group Identity in Naples," in *The Cultural Construction of Sexuality*, ed. Pat Caplan (London: Tavistock, 1987). See also Sydel Silverman, "The Life Crisis as a Clue to Social Functions," in *Anthropological Quarterly*, 40 (1967):127–138, and Carole M. Counihan, "Female Identity, Food, and Power in Contemporary Florence," in *Anthropological Quarterly*, 61 (1988):51–62.

Chapter 3. The Neapolitan Personal Style

1. Antonio Gramsci, *Letters from Prison*, transl. Lynne Lawner (New York: Harper and Row, 1973), p. 127.

Chapter 4. Tragedies of Fellowship and Community

1. Napolean Chagnon, *Yanomamö: The Fierce People* (New York: Holt, Rinehart and Winston, 1968), p. 7.

6. The Interpretation of Family Feeling ===

2. Gerald Else, *The Origin and Early Form of Greek Tragedy* (Cambridge: Harvard University Press, 1965), p. 67.

3. F. G. Friedmann, "The World of *La Miseria*," in *Peasant Society: A Reader*, ed. Jack Potter et al. (Boston: Little Brown, 1967), p. 328.

4. Gerald Suttles, *The Social Construction of Communities* (Chicago: University of Chicago Press, 1972), p. 43.

5. Miguel de Unamuno, *The Tragic Sense of Life in Men and Peoples*, transl. J. E. Crawford-Flitch (London: MacMillan and Co., 1921), p. 26.

Chapter 6. The Interpretation of Family Feeling

1. Anne Parsons, "Is the Oedipus Complex Universal?" in *The Psychoanalytic Study of Society*, ed. Warner Muensterberger and Sydney Axelrod (New York: International Universities Press, 1964).

2. Ibid.

3. Ann Cornelisen, *Women of the Shadows* (Boston: Atlantic–Little Brown, 1976).

4. See especially the study by Edward Banfield, *The Moral Basis of a Backward Society* (New York: Free Press, 1958), and the paper by Leonard Moss and Walter Thompson, "The South Italian Family: Literature and Observation," in *Human Organization*, 18 (1959): 35–41.

5. Donald Pitkin, "Land Tenure and Family Organization in an Italian Village," *Human Organization*, 18 (1959): 169–73.

6. Carol Stack, *All Our Kin* (New York: Harper and Row, 1974).

7. Sydel Silverman has criticized Banfield for not assigning causal priority to economic factors, such as prevailing patterns of land tenure, which inhibit extended families and place a ban on cooperation between families. See her paper, "Agricultural Organization, Social Structure, and Values in Italy: Amoral Familism Reconsidered," *American Anthropologist*, 70 (1968): 1–20.

8. Nancy Tanner, "Matrifocality in Indonesia and Africa and Among Black Americans," in *Women, Culture, and Society*, ed. Michelle Zimbalist Rosaldo and Louise Lamphere (Stanford: Stanford University Press, 1974), p. 131.

9. Anne Parsons, "Is the Oedipus Complex Universal?" p. 298.

10. Ann Cornelisen, *Women of the Shadows*.

11. Margaret Mead, *Sex and Temperament in Three Primitive Societies* (New York, William Morrow, 1963).

12. Bertolt Brecht, *Mother Courage and Her Children*, transl. Eric Bentley (New York: Grove Press, 1966), p. 99.

13. George Foster, "Peasant Society and the Image of Limited Good," in *Peasant Society: A Reader*, ed. Jack Potter et al. (Boston: Little Brown, 1967).

14. On family scapegoats, see Ezra Vogel and Norman Bell, "The Emotionally Disturbed Child as the Family Scapegoat," in *A Modern Introduction to the Family*, ed. Norman Bell and Ezra Vogel (Glencoe, Ill.: Free Press, 1960).

15. William S. Laughlin, "Hunting: An Integrating Bio-Behavior System and its Evolutionary Importance," in *Man the Hunter*, ed. Richard Lee and Irven DeVore (Chicago: Aldine, 1968).

195

7. The Triumvirate of Want

Chapter 7. The Triumvirate of Want

1. Fernand Braudel, *The Mediterranean and the Mediterranean World in the Age of Philip II*, vol. 1 (New York: Harper and Row, 1972), p. 347.

2. By contrast, the infant mortality rate in suburban California is 17.2 per 1000 births in the first year of life. In La Paz, Bolivia, the rate is 73 per thousand, similar to that prevailing in Naples. See Ruth Puffer and Carlos Serrano, *Patterns of Mortality in Childhood*, Publication no. 262, World Health Organization (Washington, D.C., 1973), p. 60. The Neapolitan data is taken from Gennaro Guadagno and Domenico DeMasi, eds., *La Negazione Urbana* (Bologna: Società Editrice Il Mulino, 1971), pp. 172–73.

3. Ibid.

4. Ibid., pp. 23–24.

5. Percy Allum, *Politics and Society in Post-War Naples* (Cambridge: Cambridge University Press, 1973), p. 33.

6. Antonio Vitiello, "Il genere di vita nella città di Napoli e nei suoi quartieri," in *La Negazione Urbana*, ed. Guadagno and DeMasi, p. 100.

7. A recent estimate puts the official number of unemployed at 150,000, or one-third of the work force, so that in Naples *lavoro nero*, or black labor (under-the-table enterprises and occupations), is a way of life. Indeed, according to Robert Manning, the contrabanders have now formed a union! See Robert Manning, "Italy, Politics Fester, The Economy Founders," in *Working Papers for a New Society*, May–June, 1978, p. 21.

8. Bertolt Brecht, *Mother Courage and her Children*, transl. Eric Bentley (New York: Grove Press, 1966), p. 44.

9. The reference here is to *The Immoralist*, transl. Richard Howard (New York: Random House, Vintage, 1970), p. 149.

Chapter 8. Reactions to a Disordered World

1. Michael Harrington, *Socialism* (New York: Saturday Review Press, 1970), p. 62; see also *Archives Bakouniennes*, vol. 2 (Leiden: E. J. Brill, 1957), p. xxix.

2. The poet is Robinson Jeffers, "Natural Music," *Roan Stallion, Tamar, and other Poems* (New York: Horace Liveright, 1925), p. 232.

3. Karl Marx, "A Contribution to the Critique of Hegel's Philosophy of Right." Quoted in David McLellan, *Karl Marx* (New York: Penguin, 1976), p. 29.

4. Nikolai Bukharin, *Historical Materialism: A System of Sociology* (New York: Russel and Russel, 1965), p. 290.

5. Ludwig Friedlander, *Roman Life and Manners under the Early Empire*, vol. 1 (London: Routledge, 1913), pp. 144–45.

6. Fernand Braudel, *The Mediterranean and the Mediterranean World in the Age of Philip II*, vol. 1 (New York: Harper and Row, 1972), pp. 454, 458.

7. R. M. Johnston, *The Napoleanic Empire in Southern Italy* (London: MacMillan, 1904), p. 33.

8. Giustino Fortunato, "Napoli nel 1878: La città, la plebe, le classi dirigenti," in *Territorio e Società del Mezzogiorno* (Napoli: Guida Editori, 1973), pp. 501–2.

9. Antonio Gramsci, *Selections from the Prison Notebooks of Antonio Gramsci,* ed. and transl. Quentin Hoare and G. N. Smith (London: Lawrence and Wishart, 1971), pp. 272–73.

10. Eric Hobsbawm, *Primitive Rebels* (New York: Norton, 1959); George Rudé, *The Crowd in the French Revolution* (London: Oxford University Press, 1959), and *Paris and London in the Eighteenth Century: Studies in Popular Protest* (New York: Viking Press, 1971).

11. Paul Hofman, "Food Shortages Embitter Naples," *New York Times,* December 30, 1973, p. 8.

12. Percy Allum, *Politics and Society in Post-War Naples* (Cambridge: Cambridge University Press, 1973), p. 104; Allum is here utilizing interview material gathered by L. G. Grasso.

13. Richard Sennett and Jonathan Cobb, *The Hidden Injuries of Class* (New York, Knopf, 1972).

14. James Baldwin, *Notes of a Native Son* (New York: Bantam, 1955), p. 79.

15. R. D. Laing, *The Divided Self* (London, Tavistock, 1960).

Chapter 9. Conclusion: The Poor of Naples and the World Underclass

1. Seymour Martin Lipset, "Social Class," *International Encyclopedia of the Social Sciences,* vol. 15, pp. 296–315.

2. Robert Redfield, *The Primitive World and Its Transformations* (Ithaca, N.Y.: Cornell University Press, 1953).

3. Oscar Lewis, *La Vida* (New York: Random House, 1966); see also, "The Culture of Poverty," *Scientific American,* April 1966, pp. 19–25.

4. Simone Weil, *The Iliad or the Poem of Force,* transl. Mary McCarthy (Wallingford, Pa.: Pendle Hill, 1976).

Epilogue: Return to Naples

1. For an excellent discussion of Ribera's art in its historical context, with commentaries on his paintings, see Craig Felton and William B. Jordan, eds., *Jusepe de Ribera* (Fort Worth: Kimbell Art Museum, 1982).

2. According to James Joyce, tragic art aims at exciting feelings of pity and terror. "Now terror is the feeling which arrests us before whatever is grave in human fortunes and unites us with its secret cause and pity is the feeling which arrests us before whatever is grave in human fortunes and unites us with the human sufferer." For Joyce, a work of art that moves one to prevent suffering

or take action against it is not "properly tragic." See *The Critical Writings of James Joyce*, ed. Ellsworth Mason and Richard Ellman (New York: Viking Press, 1959), pp. 141–45. For an analysis of the political and economic premises that underlie the high tradition of European oil painting, see John Berger, *Ways of Seeing* (London: Penguin, 1977).

Index

Index

200

Index

Index

202

About the Author

Photo by Christina Belmonte

Thomas Belmonte is Associate Professor of Anthropology at Hofstra Univesity.